Signal Box
Coming Up, Sir!

At Kings Cross in 1988, Class 89 electric locomotive No.89001 *The Badger* heads the 17.36 train to Peterborough. (John Cronin Collection)

Signal Box Coming Up, Sir!

AND OTHER RAILWAYMEN'S STORIES

GEOFF BODY CMILT AND BILL PARKER FCMI, FCILT, FIRO

First published 2011

The History Press
The Mill, Brimscombe Port
Stroud, Gloucestershire, GL5 2QG
www.thehistorypress.co.uk

British Library Cataloguing in Publication Data.
A catalogue record for this book is available from the British Library.

ISBN 978 0 7524 6040 6

Typesetting and origination by The History Press
Printed in Great Britain

Contents

Acknowledgements

The writers warmly record the generous and unstinting contributions made by Ian Body, Alex Bryce, Peter Caldwell, David Crathorn, John Cronin, Jim Dorward, Colin Driver, John Ellis, Jan Glasscock, the late Hugh Jenkins, Harry Knox, Mike Lamport, Don Love, Fernley Maker, Mike Phillips, Peter Rayner (from whose piece the title of this book is taken), Bill Robinson, Dennis Simmonds, Alan Sourbut, Bryan Stone, Jim Summers, Basil Tellwright, Ray Unwin, David Ward and Charles Wort – all railwaymen of great experience, noteworthy skills and immense goodwill. What they have written is, of course, based on their own views and recollections but for any failures elsewhere, blame the editor who has proved in many years of writing that however careful one tries to be some blunders always slip through. Apologies for such but hopefully they will not diminish the overall enjoyment of what has been recorded here.

Thanks are also due to those who helped and encouraged the preparation of this book in other ways and to those for whose contributions we just did not have enough space. Another time, hopefully. Meantime, thank you Allan Baker, Gerry Orbell and Peter Whittaker.

Jim Dorward kindly did the drawings and the other illustrations are from the editor's collection except where specifically recorded. Colin Brown provided valuable help and support in the preparation of the final work.

The positive input and support provided by Amy Rigg and Emily Locke of The History Press has been invaluable.

Blame the Parents

A Sort of Introduction

Editor Geoff Body's father was a railwayman, his wife ran St Neots booking office and both Geoff and his son were railway traffic apprentices. Bill Parker, the compiler and another TA, had a talent for mathematics but, following the example of his father who was a widely experienced station and yard master, chose a career that was destined to lead him to the post of divisional manager at Kings Cross.

I 'blame' my father, 'Jim' Body, if blame is the right word. Certainly he was largely responsible for priming me for a railway career, but it was to provide me with so much interest and satisfaction that gratitude is really a more appropriate sentiment. He it was who took six-year-old me down to Peterborough North station to see silver-grey A4 streamlined Pacific No.2509 *Silver Link* head the press run of the inaugural Silver Jubilee train on 27 September 1935. Just 110 years since the Stockton & Darlington Railway had begun its passenger service, *Silver Link* broke four world records on this run, including achieving 112.5mph twice.

In the memoirs I persuaded him to write in later years, my father appears to have broken a record of his own on one occasion. After being taken on by the Great Northern Railway as a lad trainee at Great Ponton in 1916, he was soon moved to Waddington to help cope with the large volume of materials arriving for the new aerodrome there. His salary went up from 9s to 12s 6d a week but his lodgings cost 15s so he continued to need parental subsidy. Just as he left the station one night a German Zeppelin passed low overhead searching for a train to bomb. When a dark shape dropped from the airship above him, Dad broke his own personal sprint record only to find when the shock had passed that the menace was just an empty fuel can!

At the other end of the scale of experiences my father provided, but one equally vividly remembered, was a visit to Stamford East station when Dad was relieving there. What a place of enchantment. The main station buildings, elaborate and pleasing in their warm Barnack stone, were in the style of the Marquis of Exeter's Burghley House, unsurprising for the short branch line to Essendine had originally been largely funded by the second marquis. Inside the square booking hall the various rooms around the circulating area had their own gallery at first-floor level to create a very imposing, almost baronial, impression before entry to the platform area, quite dark beneath its low canopy and totally mysterious and exciting. Being then admitted onto the footplate of the branch

Seen here in 1966, thirteen years after its last passenger train, the ornate station at Stamford East is being used by a household removals firm.

locomotive made quite sure that, for me, the whole experience would be unforgettable.

Going with my father into the passimeter booking office at Peterborough East when he was working a Saturday late shift gave me a real sense of being part of this vast and exciting world that was then the London & North Eastern Railway. I saw less of Dad during the war as he was away a lot with a dedicated police squad chasing black marketeers, but the seed had been sown in my formative years and, without thought of further education, I became a 'Temporary Probationary Junior Male Clerk' at St Neots station in September 1945.

Like myself and many other railwaymen, my co-writer, Bill Parker, benefited greatly from the considerable experience and ability of his father. To use his words:

From a child I 'lived' railways at home, going frequently 'to help' in Peterborough North booking office and New England yard master's office where my father was a clerk. And as a teenager I continued the practice in the passenger and goods offices where my father was a relief station master in the Kings Cross district and then station master/goods agent at Stairfoot, Mexborough and Welwyn Garden City, and a Doncaster assistant yard master.

I was permitted – and hardly discouraged – to attend derailments and observe the rerailing of the vehicles and the infrastructure repairs. Under strict supervision I regularly operated signal boxes, acted as pilotman in single line working, and also became quite accomplished with a shunting pole. Moreover, I became more conversant with the rule book and the block signalling regulations than with some of my school certificate subjects!

I was, nonetheless, at that time destined to have a career in the financial accountancy industry, but I found at my fifth grammar school that I was very behind in two of my subjects needed for the higher school certificate. Much to the annoyance of the head and maths masters, I decided to leave school and join the railway, which appeared at the time to have very interesting prospects, with all the talk in the air of impending nationalisation and integration of inland transport. My father did not try to influence me in my decision, although I knew he was extremely pleased when I started in the Doncaster district operating superintendent's office (despite being in the staff office and not in the trains office!) and he continued to be a wonderful guide and mentor, and a tower of strength, in my early railway positions.

Although I would most probably have earned much more money in the financial world, I question whether I would have had the great enjoyment, fun and satisfaction I derived from working on the railway, particularly in some of the most rewarding jobs – relief station master, district inspector, divisional operating superintendent and divisional manager – and from working with such professionals and experiencing the companionship of a superb group of people of all grades and departments – called railwaymen and women.

Railwaymen are in the conveyance business, moving goods and people with a product that is perishable in the sense that unfilled space is costly and wasted. To do the job well an understanding of both product and customers is critical, which to us meant travelling on one's own trains even under adverse circumstances such as the wildly swinging brake van of an express meat train, and going down mines or into cement works to appreciate the factors which formulated your freight client's requirements. Again this produced its own indelible memories, like the sheer primeval power of the crushers used on Mendip stone before loading to block trains at Merehead Quarry.

David Ward, another traffic apprentice, summed up his own experience by writing:

> Front line railway work involved 24 hours of the day, seven days a week, and was often carried out in bad weather or uncongenial conditions. To ensure the reliability, safety and punctuality of the train service required a very high standard of personal discipline and teamwork. It was no place for the work-shy or those of fragile temperament. It bred a workforce of characters to whom good humour was part of the scene, men who were always prepared to pass on their experience...

Add on the delights and challenges of varied and complex equipment, varied and complex situations and varied and complex people and it is little wonder that a railway career produces a host of notable experiences and memories, a flavour of which former schoolmate and colleague Bill Parker and I have tried to capture here. By enlisting the help of others we have met and enjoyed working with, we have sought to record a selection of the very best of their experiences and our own, and to present them here in a true professional setting, and in the hope that the end product proves as fascinating to the reader as it has to its compilers.

Getting the Sack

When, after joining the LNER, Geoff Body finished his induction period there was no immediate vacancy for him, so he was given the task of trying to recover 44,000 missing railway sacks.

When I joined the London & North Eastern Railway in 1945, I was sent for a period of training at St Neots station on the East Coast Main Line. This area was highly fertile with farming and market gardening the main occupations, along with the ancillary activities which supplied and supported them. Each clerk in the booking and goods offices cheerfully shared their knowledge and experience with me and even forgave my naivety when I innocently told the auditors that if we had a surplus in the daily cash balance we put it in the tea fund tin!

One of my mentors was Joan Peck who had a small office of her own among the platform buildings and was in charge of 'Sacks'. Up to this point I had no idea that the railway companies owned thousands of sacks which were hired out to farmers to encourage the movement of their grain harvests by rail. The provision of a supply of sacks was free if they were used for forwarding by rail and then returned within a stipulated time. If not, a time-based penalty charge was raised. Supporting this activity on the LNER was a whole department under the control of the sack superintendent at Lincoln where there was also a factory for making and repairing the sacks, all of which were branded with the railway's initials.

There was no vacant post for me when my training period was over, so I was sent to neighbouring Sandy station to tackle a problem which had clearly been building for some time. The office of the district goods & passenger manager at Peterborough contacted the St Neots station master, Archie Mehew, who in turn let me know that Sandy seemed to have mislaid around 44,000 sacks which had been issued but not returned. I was to have the challenge (and privilege!) of transferring to the former LMS goods office at Sandy and sorting the whole matter out. Basically this meant either getting the sacks back or making someone pay for them.

Fortunately Joan, who had taught me the little I knew about the sack business, was actually the wife of a farmer and had been able to reveal some of the many pitfalls that my new task would present. Having a Lincolnshire farming background myself, I could see some of the potential difficulties. All of my fears, and several more, proved well founded. Farmers around Sandy clearly had better things to do than keep records of sacks.

The first response to an enquiry about the whereabouts of some missing sacks was to deny ever having had them. When a signed receipt for their issue was unearthed, the collection was suddenly remembered along with the fact that the sacks were definitely used to send grain by rail. Surely the consignee had returned them, but perhaps they got lost on the railway somewhere. If not, we should contact the consignee and let our farmer get on with his urgent farm business. Had he, perhaps, mistakenly used the sacks for a load which had been carried by road transport? Mostly certainly not!

If we could not trace ever having a grain forwarding from our farmer and duly said so, communications between us suddenly seemed to fail. At that time we were only allowed to use the GPO telephone system sparingly but it was little use anyway for whenever I called the farmer was either at market, dealing with a sick cow or away pulling a tractor out of a ditch some miles distant. On the rare occasions that I struck lucky it was to be told blithely, 'Oh, those sacks. Sorry, but the rats ate them.'

By the time I moved on from Sandy I had managed to cut the problem down by half.

It had been an interesting period when I had learned as much about human nature as I had about the railway sack business. There had been other compensations too, for a small mobile platform canteen left over from serving wartime troop exchanges between the main line and the Bletchley–Cambridge line was still functioning and serving sandwiches, cakes and tea. Sandy was also where I met my future wife!

LNER 5517/9/45—6,000   G. 739

LONDON AND NORTH EASTERN RAILWAY.

GOODS DEPARTMENT.

....Station.

Telephone No......................

.... 194.....

Reference :

....

Dear Sir,

(1) On.............................194...., you

hired from this Station...............................

L.N.E.R. Sacks ....

which have not been returned here.

(2) M...

of ....

transfer...........................L.N.E.R. sacks to

you on and from.............................194.....

    Will you please complete the annexed card showing how the sacks have been disposed of, and return to me.

    Yours faithfully,

PENNY STAMP

PRINTED PAPER.

THE ADDRESS TO BE WRITTEN ON THIS SIDE.

REPLY.

LONDON & NORTH EASTERN RAILWAY.

GOODS DEPARTMENT.

A standard LNER form of enquiry about sacks hired, but not returned.

Never Work with Animals!

Bill Robinson's early railway years introduced him to 'Livestock by Rail' and the fact that animals have a character all their own.

Amongst my first memories on joining the railway late in December 1959 was the sack business that Geoff Body has described. As a young, probationary clerk I spent my first few weeks in the goods office at Driffield in East Yorkshire. It was a busy office with six people working on all aspects of freight traffic. One person stood out; he was the sack clerk who spent his days toiling over the accounts, calculating sack hire at the rate of one penny farthing per week per sack. His calculations were done with a pencil which was near the end of its life, but he kept it going by inserting it into a metal tube so as to use the last of the lead, a hangover from wartime economy measures. The sack clerk's appearance matched his work. It was a cold winter and he wore knitted gloves with his fingers exposed. He always seemed to have a long dewdrop on the end of his nose! Later the sack business was sold to East Riding Sacks whose lorries you can still see to this day, providing a link with a long-lost aspect of railways.

Six weeks later I moved down the line to Beverley where I was to learn the skills of a booking clerk. This was where I was introduced to the railway livestock business.

The most common example of livestock handled was the pigeon traffic. During the racing season fanciers would bring their baskets of birds to the station where they would be weighed and charged for despatch to the chosen destination station. On arrival there the platform staff would release the birds and endorse the label with the release time before sending the basket back to Beverley. By checking the time of arrival at the pigeon loft back home the fancier could monitor the performance of his birds. This process continued throughout the season with the birds being sent progressively further away in preparation for the races ahead. On the eve of a race the fanciers would then bring in their selected birds for the baskets to be forwarded on a special 'pigeon train'. So important was this business to the LNER that they built special vans with racks to hold the baskets.

On occasions, some time after a race, a scruffy cardboard box would arrive marked 'Livestock'. It would contain a pigeon and the fancier would be advised that we had an item for collection. On one occasion when he came to collect the bird I asked, 'What will you do with it?' Without hesitation came the reply, 'Wring its bloody neck. It's no good to me if it can't find its way home!'

Whilst pigeons were frequent travellers, they were not the only birds to go by rail. Newly hatched chicks would arrive for farmers and smallholders, carried in cardboard boxes provided with air holes through which emerged a chorus of constant chirping. Budgerigars for breeders would come in smaller boxes, similar ones occasionally arriving containing a single mouse – a super stud, perhaps!

Livestock did not only travel in boxes. Once a calf arrived in the guard's van, all bound in hessian sacking, and had to be carried out to the farmer's truck. It seems unlikely that this would be permitted today. Other animals would arrive tethered in the brake van, including dogs coming to kennels and rams arriving for sheep farmers. One particularly fine specimen of the latter arrived off the York train for transfer to the Bridlington line. The parcels porter led it by the rope and all went well until the platform end when the ram just stopped. No amount of encouraging and pulling could move it. So the porter went round to its back end and squeezed in a tender area. The ram then proceeded like a lamb to make its forward connection. This was for me a powerful and wider lesson for the future!

Horses travelled in style in their own horsebox attached to local passenger trains. In the booking office we would receive a telegram telling us of the impending arrival so that we could tell the signal box and platform staff. The horsebox would then be detached and placed by the train engine in the cattle dock for unloading. The train would then resume its journey 10 to 15 minutes late. No Government punctuality targets in those days!

Some five years later found me appointed as assistant yard master at York. Once again I became involved with livestock, this time cattle. Irish cattle would arrive in the early hours accompanied by a drover to see to their welfare. It was to be my job to check them before their forward journey. One of my fellow AYMs gave me some advice on this aspect of my duties. 'Walk along the wagons and look to see if any of the beasts are on the floor. If they are, get the drover and he will sort it out. If, while you are doing this, you hear a clapping noise, run away fast.'

'Why?' I asked.

'It means a cow is relieving itself against the wagon side and you will be lucky to avoid getting covered.' That was another lesson about management – when the muck is flying you will need luck or experience to avoid it!

My other livestock experience at York was more exotic. It was the circus train. I was on duty one Sunday morning and walked down Holgate Dock to see if all was well. The leading vehicles carried elephants which spent much of their time using their trunks to pull closed the double doors. As they continued to move about the doors would swing open again and the whole process was repeated. When this bored them they would suck up dust from the dock with their trunks and blow it all over themselves.

There were further vans and horseboxes from which the circus staff unloaded horses, camels and llamas. A keeper asked me to hold on to one llama while he dealt with another. All I knew of these creatures was that they were given to spitting so, as a precaution, I kept its head as far from me as possible. Before long the llama began jumping up and down. 'What's the matter with it?' I asked. 'Look, maister,' said the keeper, 'If you were standing in that bed of nettles without your trousers on, you'd be jumping about!'

By mid-morning the yard master appeared and asked, 'What's happening, Bill?' I gave him a short rundown on the events of the day just as we arrived at the elephant van. They were still happily powdering themselves with dust from the dock. 'Dirty beggars,' was my boss's comment, whereupon one elephant promptly blew dust all over him. The moral of this incident was that there is no such thing as a dumb animal.

In the light of these experiences I sought out any official guidance I could get, for I feared I might be faced with having to milk a cow. The answer I found in a BTC booklet entitled *Livestock on Rail*. I read the section on milking cows. It began:

> First of all you must gain the cow's confidence by approaching its head. Talk to it and stroke its head and neck. Continue talking to it, gradually stroking the back. If the cow is still untroubled move down its sides, all the while talking to it. Then feel the udder and start milking.

Readers may wonder what lessons I learned from this for my future career!

That, alas, was my last dealing with animals on rail except that when joining the Royal Train one night at Kings Cross I was surprised to see a Jack Russell terrier running down the corridor! But that is not part of this story.

Up, Up and Away

Colin Driver, too, learned something from the livestock business quite early in his career.

Having joined the railways as a booking clerk at Worthing in the early 1950s, I had still to learn about the wonders of BR pigeon specials. The South Coast of the Southern Region had to content itself with carrying individual baskets of pigeons on its passenger trains. The pigeon fancier would bring a basket to the station with a label attached showing the train to be despatched by. The time that the bird had to be released by staff at the destination station was also shown.

On a quiet Sunday morning, our regular fancier arrived at West Worthing parcels office with his basket containing one of his widely travelled pigeons. The labelling was clear, the bird was destined for Steyning, with a change at Shoreham-by-Sea. There was no excuse for the subsequent failure.

Later on that Sunday my colleague and I noticed, to our horror, that the basket was still on the parcels office counter. We had forgotten to give it to the platform staff to despatch by the designated train... and we could not complain about the workload on that particular Sunday as an excuse! There was no later train to Steyning that would leave before the release time. What should we do? Our station master would not be pleased to get a complaint on Monday morning.

My colleague suggested that he telephone 'a knowledgeable pigeon friend' and get some idea of the flying time from Steyning back to Worthing. This enabled us to work out what time to release the pigeon that was still sitting on the parcels counter. Fortunately there were no sophisticated timing devices for flights in those days. But would the idea work?

We had to wait for a fortnight before our pigeon fancier arrived at Worthing station again with one of his baskets. With some trepidation, we asked how things had gone two weeks before. His reply, 'Well, he arrived back at my pigeon loft at about the expected time, but there was one really strange thing. The bird was not even panting after flying from Steyning.' That was not surprising to us, as West Worthing station was only round the corner from his house!

I wonder – would I have ever experienced the delights of being BR's Director, Freight, if the idea had failed and the truth had come out? Later, an experienced and knowledgeable secretary suggested that the story was an early example of the low cunning required by all railway managers!

Footplate Adventure

Harry Knox vividly remembers firing A3 No.60098 *Spion Kop* on an exhilarating working with the Talisman express from Edinburgh to Newcastle and back.

Having joined British Railways in 1956 as a junior clerk at Shotts (Lanarks), the daily routine of, in the morning, waybilling coal consigned to rail from four local collieries, and in the afternoon covering the booking office between the early and late shift booking clerks, quickly began to pall. To me this was not the real railway and so I applied to transfer to Edinburgh Haymarket Motive Power Depot as an engine cleaner. The transfer was approved, and on my seventeenth birthday, early in 1957, I became one of some 130 cleaners on the strength at the shed.

In the winter months, the cleaners were split into three gangs on rotating shifts and Haymarket engines were thoroughly cleaned. After about six weeks, I was taken out by the firing instructor on a Class A3 locomotive, working the 08.05 Edinburgh to Thornton, and had to fire the engine under his eagle eye and that of the regular driver. The return journey was made on a Dundee to Edinburgh passenger train worked by Dundee men, and the Dundee fireman was quite happy to go back 'on the cushions' whilst I worked his train forward to destination. This was repeated on the following day, and on the third day I was taken in front of the shed master and examined orally in technical knowledge and Rules & Regulations and was, in due course, 'passed out' for firing duties as a passed cleaner.

By mid-April, the depot holiday roster kicked in and more senior cleaners were soon being booked out firing. As the year moved into May, more and more cleaners went out as firemen until the junior men, myself included, began to have odd days on the firing roster. Essentially, these firing turns were on local pilots or on shed duties, such as preparation and disposal, and were all good experience. However, whilst it was policy to keep younger passed cleaners away from main line work, sometimes being in the right place at the right time meant that main line turns were forthcoming. Thus it was that I, in the early summer, found myself firing a V2 on the 16.00 Edinburgh to Inverness passenger train, as far as Perth. An adventure indeed!

The summer moved on and more firing turns were coming my way, but mainly on a day-to-day basis. One or two main line turns were an unexpected bonus. By October, with the summer timetable finished and with the depot holiday roster ending, it was back to cleaning duties until the next spring.

In 1958, being somewhat more senior, I found that, by the summer, I was firing for whole weeks at a time, and the opportunity to swap turns was now a reality. Because late turns of duty suited me from a travel point of view, I found many regular firemen were amenable to exchanging unsocial late shifts or night turns for day turns of duties. Through this process, I found myself firing to a top link driver on his allocated A4 locomotive No.60004 *William Whitelaw*, on the Down Aberdonian, the 03.57 Edinburgh to Dundee sleeping car train, with an ungodly booking-on time of 02.00. This I worked for the full week although the driver, one Bob Proudfoot, made quite a fuss on the first morning when I appeared as his fireman and a locomotive inspector had to travel with us. All went well and I completed the week without incident.

The new year, 1959, dawned and again I was cleaning in the early months, but come late April was soon back out firing again. It really was more of the same and at Haymarket, with so many big locomotives allocated, preparation duties could be arduous to say the least. As the year moved on diesel locomotives were appearing, and it was becoming clear that the days of the firemen were now numbered. Nevertheless, I enjoyed the variety of work and working some more main line turns.

Towards the end of July that year, I found myself rostered 15.00 'Junior Spare' for a whole week, this link covering all sorts of turns as required. On the Thursday, on checking the daily working sheets, I found I had been elevated to the 15.00 'Senior Spare' turn the following day, the 'Senior Spare'

A4 No.60004 *William Whitelaw* is pictured in front of Haymarket shed in 1959. The author had fired this engine for Driver Proudfoot on the Aberdonian sleeper the previous year. (W. Hermiston/Transport Treasury)

covering any and all train working turns as required. On taking duty on the Friday, the running foreman advised me to make myself known to No.3 link driver, P.B. Robertson.

Now Peter Robertson was one of the great speed merchants at Haymarket and I was now to be his fireman on the 16.00 Edinburgh to London Kings Cross, The Talisman, then one of the East Coast crack expresses, which we were booked to work to Newcastle, some 125 miles to the south, in an allotted running time of 126 minutes. We then worked the northbound service back later in the day, 256 miles of express running all round.

I joined Peter at the notice cases, and found that we had been allocated a Gresley Pacific Class A3 locomotive, No.60098 *Spion Kop*, one of our own, for this turn of duty. Now this A3 was then thirty years old but, thanks to both the persistence of Peter Townend, shed master, King's Cross Top Shed, in eventually getting all the Gresley Pacifics fitted with the Kylchap exhaust arrangement and double chimneys, which transformed the steaming ability and free running, and also to the innovative introduction of optical aligning equipment at Doncaster by K.J. Cook, plus a modified design of middle big end on the engines, many of the former weaknesses in the design had been laid to rest and the A3s and A4s were given a new lease of life. On that afternoon No.60098 had just been through Doncaster Shops for general repair and sported a new double chimney. After a quick check round, we phoned 'Off Shed' and, on receiving the exit signal, slowly made our way down to Waverley station and coupled up to our train, a limited load of nine coaches, all roller-bearing fitted, weighing 307 tons tare/320 gross.

Driver Peter Robertson (on the right) and Fireman John Wilson in front of A1 No.60161 *North British* at Edinburgh Haymarket shed, prior to working the Up Queen of Scots Pullman in April 1956. (J. Robertson/Transport Treasury)

On the dot of 16.00 whistles blew and a green flag was waved at the rear of the train. Peter quickly had it on the move, although the start southwards from Edinburgh was easy, with a falling gradient of 1 in 78 for the first mile. There was a permanent speed restriction of 35mph for the 7 miles to Monktonhall Junction so I was able to sit in comfort watching the world go by. As we cleared Monktonhall, the regulator was opened right up and the blast took effect on the fire. I started firing, little and often in the approved fashion. The train was tightly timed but I had no difficulty keeping steam pressure at around 220lb/sq.in. and the boiler three quarters full of water.

We raced across the East Lothian plain and soon the brakes went on to steady progress for the Dunbar curves. We swept southwards and on to the 1 in 200 gradient up towards Oxwellmains and the precursor to the 5-mile climb up the 1 in 96 gradient through the Lammermuir Hills to Grantshouse summit. I eased my firing as the top of the climb was passed, and was thereafter able to make good use of the padded bucket seats so thoughtfully provided by Sir Nigel Gresley for his trainmen, firing only a couple of times before we rushed down along the Berwickshire sea cliffs, crossing over the border into Northumberland, and on through Berwick upon Tweed station. We swung over the Royal Border Bridge and I enjoyed the panoramic view over the town and the North Sea, brilliantly and enticingly blue on this fine summer afternoon.

Once clear of Tweedmouth we accelerated over the small rise at Spittal and dropped down the falling gradient through Scremerston to Goswick. Firing was light and often and no problems were being experienced with an engine in prime condition. Approaching Lucker I prepared to drop the water scoop at the troughs there and shut off the injector in readiness. At a shout from Peter, I wound the scoop down, and as water began to show in the 'walking stick' indicator the scoop was withdrawn, with difficulty. Some 2,000 gallons of water had been lifted! We ran on towards Newcastle and the 40mph speed restriction round the severe Morpeth curve was strictly observed. Passing Benton Bank signal box, I pushed the remaining fire forward and closed the firehole flap, and we drifted down through Heaton and crashed our way over the immense set of diamond crossings, to come to a stand in Newcastle Central at 18.03, some 3 minutes early. It had been an uneventful trip with an engine in first class order and I had had no problems with either steam or water. I reckoned I had shovelled around 2½ tons of coal. However, the real adventure was still to come!

Having been uncoupled from the train, we ran forward over the King Edward Bridge and into Gateshead shed where we were relieved and our engine taken for fire cleaning, coaling and preparation. Gateshead shed was an interesting place and, because of its location, turning the engine to head northwards was never required. After having our meal break, we once again took over No.60098 and, having phoned out to the signalman at Greenfields Junction, we were signalled out, chimney leading, southwards, only to be signalled back over the High Level Bridge, now tender leading and ready to couple on to our train in Newcastle Central Station. Our back working to Edinburgh was the northbound Talisman, the 16.00 ex-King's Cross, due to leave Newcastle at 20.34.

We were held on the High Level Bridge awaiting arrival of the northbound service, watching life pass below us on the River Tyne, and as we waited Peter explained his strategy for the northbound leg of the journey. He indicated that, after a small dip between the Central station and Manors, we were faced with a 5-mile climb up to Forest Hall, by which point it was his intention to have reached at least 60mph, and thus we would be 'working against the collar' to achieve this. He also explained his technique for timing this train over the 125 miles to Edinburgh and, with only 126 minutes allowed, there was no room for error. Peter relished the challenge posed by late starts, having an impressive record of on-time arrivals under such circumstances. Little did I know what was in store!

Sitting on our lofty perch above the Tyne, we had a clear view of the King Edward Bridge upriver, and so could see our train as it approached from the south. The incoming Talisman came into view at 20.38, and a late start was now on the cards. It was not until around 20.42 that the King's Cross A4 which had worked the train from London slid past us on the bridge, and we were signalled back into the station and onto the train. Coupled up and brake test carried out, I now fired some coal into the box and put on the blower. A haze of grey smoke hit the station roof. Away back along the train, a green flag was waved and whistles blew. Peter pulled open the regulator and 60098 had the train on the move without any fuss, but now 12 minutes late. With the cut-off set at 35 per cent, Peter pulled the regulator fully open as we cleared Manors platforms and *Spion Kop* shouted her way up through Heaton. At Heaton shed men paused to watch us roar past on the climb up to Forest Hall. I was now firing almost continuously, pausing only to check water levels and sweep the floor at regular intervals.

We blazed away up the hill and as we swept past Forest Hall at a speed just in excess of the planned 60mph, Peter gave me the thumbs up. We had 20½ minutes allowed to pass Morpeth (16.60 miles) with its 40mph speed restriction, and thus there was no let up, although the reverser was pulled back to around 20 per cent. We hit the eighties at Stannington before the brakes went on for Morpeth, and we cleared the platform there having taken just 18 minutes from Newcastle. Peter had regained 3 minutes and I knew now that I was in for a rough trip.

We hammered away towards Alnmouth, with another speed restriction of 60mph looming because of the left-hand curve through the station, and passed Alnmouth signal box in 33 minutes – 4 minutes now clawed back. Up the 1 in 170 climb to Little Mill and at the 309 milepost we went over the top and on to Christon Bank. This was one of the fastest pieces of railway between Newcastle and Edinburgh, and Peter was taking full advantage. Down the bank we raced and speed rose into the nineties at Chathill. Again, speed had to be steadied because of the troughs at Lucker and we picked up water at a sedate 60mph before accelerating away again over the relatively level Northumberland plain and Embleton Moss.

Belford (51.65 miles) was passed in 46 minutes with 6 minutes now regained, and by Beal we had again hit the nineties before climbing once

A3 No.60098 *Spion Kop* is the engine the author fired two months earlier when 12 minutes were recovered on the Down Talisman between Newcastle and Edinburgh. (W. Hermiston/ Transport Treasury)

more to go over the top at Spittal and on through Berwick. With 69½ minutes allowed, we were through Berwick in 3 minutes over the even hour, and passed Marshall Meadows signal box, and into Scotland, still a mere 6 minutes adrift. Up along the 1 in 190 rising gradient along the sea cliffs, Peter let her out to 30 per cent cut off through Burnmouth, and by Reston (79.20 miles) we were only 3 minutes late. Grantshouse (83.30 miles) was passed in 76 minutes, and Dunbar in 86 minutes. Some fast running over the East Lothian plain saw the high eighties being reached at Longniddry, and Monktonhall Junction (118.35 miles) was passed in 105 minutes against the 117 allowed. A clear road (most unusual) at Portobello East Junction meant that we pulled into Edinburgh Waverley bang on time at 22.40, having recovered all 12 minutes, and running the 125 miles in 114 minutes net. I calculated that on the return journey at least some 3 tons of coal had gone into the firebox. Quite a journey and quite an adventure for a young fireman!

The First Day...
A Rare Initiation

On Bill Parker's first day as a relief station master he was just congratulating himself that the morning had gone quite well when the mood was shattered by the news of a derailment on his patch.

It was early 1950s. I was twenty-one and three quarters years of age, and had been appointed to the lowly post of summer relief station master, Class 5 grade, in the Doncaster District of British Railways. My first day in the new post was to be the start of several weeks as station master at a couple of adjoining small stations, Dodworth and Silkstone, on the route between Barnsley Court House and Penistone. Finally the appointed day arrived along with the challenging realisation that I was going to be in charge. I recall my feelings as a mix of the confidence and exuberance of youth, interspersed by shreds of trepidation.

Not that I was unprepared. I had learned a great deal from my father's long and varied experience in station master and assistant yard master posts. I had acquired a lot of practical knowledge – some of it quite unofficially – and had passed a number of examinations in railway subjects including the highly satisfying achievement of a first class certificate in Rules & Regulations, and passing the lengthy oral examination by the chief district inspector. Now it had all to be put to work.

Following my father's practice of being on the station platforms during the morning and evening 'peak' times, I had arrived at Dodworth on an early train at about 7.15a.m., met the booking clerk and telephoned Silkstone to check the situation there. In my somewhat ill-fitting dark blue uniform suit and proudly wearing my gold-braided station master's cap, I had set off on a tour of my new empire, complimenting the platform porter on the waiting rooms and toilets which were impeccably clean and tidy, and then moving on to the signal box where the signalman greeted me with a very welcome mug of strong, sweet tea and the information that the morning train service to Barnsley was, as usual, late. According to the foreman at Penistone this was the fault of unworkable engine and traincrew diagrams and rosters so a call to Griff Griffiths, my previous boss in Doncaster passenger trains office, was going to be needed later in the day.

Armed with information about the late running trains, I then ventured onto the Up platform only to be surrounded by some thirty or forty angry passengers, who were somewhat taken aback to see a station master at that time of the morning, and a young whippersnapper at that. I was immediately accosted by their spokesman, a solicitor well over 6ft tall and nearly twice my weight, who vehemently expressed complaints about the whole train service and lack of information, and wanted to know in very strong language what I was going to do about it. I did manage to explain the action I intended to take, but cynical comments from the solicitor suggested he didn't believe me! The whole event had been my first experience of customer relations.

By sheer good fortune we found a way of improving passenger communication by using a loudhailer borrowed by the porter from one of his soccer pals – for use Mondays to Fridays only as it had to be back on the trainer's bench for matches on Saturdays! This rather basic aid to good communication would be used by the signalman from his lofty position at the top of the signal box steps.

Having faced up to the weighty solicitor, I next dealt with a group of rowdy students from Barnsley Grammar School who showed little respect either for my gold braid or their own safety. I had to challenge their running about on the platform and the barrow crossing.

The 'morning peak' over, I spent some time in the various offices. Once the shock of my youth had passed, the elderly but very experienced clerks seemed to be taking the same view as the senior civil servants in TV's *Yes, Minister*, i.e. 'provided he behaves himself, he may be alright'. Next came a tour of the goods shed activities and those in the yard and colliery sidings and the signal box where, at all places, I enjoyed a more overt acceptance from the conciliation staff, probably because I could work the signal box, manhandle some parcels and goods sundries, and hold my own with a shunting pole.

After a very substantial high-calorie canteen lunch with the local colliery manager, I sat in my office awaiting the arrival of the light engine to take me to Silkstone. I had heard from Griff that the diagrams and rosters would be changed from next Monday to improve the morning trains' punctuality and, looking back, I could not help thinking that the day had gone pretty well so far and indulging in a small measure of satisfaction on what I had done and, indeed, feeling rather relaxed about the job.

This was clearly a major mistake. My short moment of complacency was rudely shattered by the unceremonious intrusion of the booking clerk whose whole demeanour suggested 'disaster'. And so it proved. He had received an urgent message from the signalman at West Silkstone Junction that two freight trains had collided and there was a 'so-and-so' big pile up, all lines were blocked, and some of the train crew were injured.

'Don't panic, don't panic!' – not exactly emulating Lance Corporal Jones of TV's *Dad's Army*, but, fighting down a feeling of apprehension, I contacted the signalman to check that an ambulance had been sent for, that all lines approaching the obstruction had or were being protected by detonators, that the 'six bells' obstruction danger signal had been sent to all the adjoining signal boxes, and that Doncaster District Control had been informed; and was told with great clarity to the effect that 'of course they had'.

I then contacted the control office myself and had it confirmed that all trains currently on the three routes towards West Silkstone Junction had been stopped *pro tem*, that arrangements were in hand for an emergency bus service between Barnsley Court House and Penistone stations, stopping at my intermediate stations, and that all the engineering departments were being informed. I told the deputy chief controller that I intended to go immediately to the accident scene.

A quick word with the booking clerk made sure that Dodworth and Silkstone passengers would be kept informed about the situation and my successful efforts to improve the morning services, and that he would oversee the use of the temporary bus service. I told the signalmen at Silkstone station and West Silkstone Junction signal boxes that I would be coming to the accident site on a light engine, and then headed for the light engine which had now arrived at Dodworth.

At Silkstone we picked up a wrong line order in case the light engine had to return in the wrong direction, the signalman reminding me to take a clamp for the catch points in the Down line. After some muttering from the driver concluding with the comment, 'all reet, thar's in't charge!' we got to the Junction signal without any more murmurings. There, my first thoughts were, of course, about the condition of the injured. These proved to be the driver and fireman of the Up line train from Mottram marshalling yard to Wath marshalling yard, the engine of which had become derailed across the junction points and was leaning some 20/25 degrees towards the Wath to Mottram train on the Down line. They had been thrown across the footplate and were receiving first-aid treatment by the driver and guard of the Down line train, both of whom were unharmed. These two were using their St John's Ambulance training and doing an excellent job that earned them a most complimentary pat on the back when the ambulance crew arrived and took over.

In the Junction signal box I was greeted by a mature and rather overweight signalman, who had clearly heard about me working the Dodworth box that morning and, with a broad grin, asked in a broad South Yorkshire accent, 'Thars not cum t'work t'box, has't thee? Thar's too late!', and handed me a large mug of sweet tea. He seemed a bit nonplussed when I checked and recorded the position of the block indicators and the position of the levers in the frame, noting his entries recording the situation in the train register book, and that the semaphore signal for the Up train was still in the off position.

As one would expect from such an experienced signalman he was able to give me a detailed account of what had happened, stating that both freight trains were running on clear signals to and from the heavily used freight-only Worsborough branch and that, in his view, the speed of the derailed train crossing the junction towards the branch was quite normal. He had been watching the train movements and said that as the engine of the Up line train from Mottram was actually passing the junction facing points there was a loud noise followed by dust rising from beneath the engine. It then lurched and continued to run off the track towards the Worsborough branch, coming to a stand near the middle of the passing Down train which consisted entirely of wagons loaded with steel. The Up derailed train comprised empty open coal wagons only, the first ten of which had followed the engine off the track, two of them becoming uncoupled and ending up resting on the steel wagons of the Down line train.

My own observation confirmed the state of the engine and wagons and considerable damage around the junction to the track and signalling. With this clear picture of the situation in my mind I passed on all the information I had to the control office where the deputy chief controller confirmed that arrangements were being made to clear all the other trains already in the area and that everyone had been told of the emergency bus service being laid on. He had alerted all the

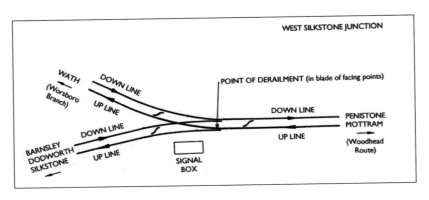

engineering departmental heads and was able to tell me that the steam cranes at Doncaster and Mexborough locomotive sheds were being prepared, along with Gorton Shed's heavy steam crane for dealing with the Penistone side of the accident. The Mexborough shed master and his breakdown foreman were on their way by van to assess the precise breakdown crane requirements.

Next I had an inwards phone call from my boss, the assistant district operating superintendent, wanting to be updated and then telling me that both the local district inspector and the Barnsley station master were off sick so I was to take charge operationally. I was, he said, to work closely with the senior staff of the other departments involved but not to 'let them to get away with murder' – undefined! Frankly, I was delighted with his decision to leave me in charge.

In the event we set up an extremely good liaison system and, after an inspection by the district civil engineer of the track outside the damaged area, and an inspection of the un-derailed wagons by the district carriage & wagon engineer, everything that was moveable was moved. I was in regular contact with the inspector at Penistone and the various signalmen and others involved, reminding everyone about the catch points and the normal trailing points which would be facing for the reverse movements. All of these would be clamped and hand-signalled by the platelayers provided by the permanent way inspector.

I had, on my arrival at the site, taken possession of the lines on all sides of West Silkstone Junction, everyone understanding that no movement must be made without my authority. This course of action had the full support of the breakdown train foremen and the district civil engineer as it gave more flexibility during the re-railing processes and track repairs. I felt reassured by my actions when the assistant district operating superintendent confirmed them on his arrival, as the signalman at the junction had initially queried them as he had never seen this done before except for engineering possessions. However, he had accepted the position, adding, 'If thar wants to ben't rules, thar can; thar knows what thar's doing and thar's sign't book, so it's alreet wi me!'

Understandably, because railwaymen instinctively rally round during emergencies, the site had become a mass of senior staff of all the engineering disciplines involved. My boss needed to get back to Doncaster quickly but approved what had been done and confirmed that I should remain in control until my relief turned up sometime next morning. Before he left, I joined him and the engineers in a preliminary review of the accident based on the initial statements obtained by questioning the available train crews and the signalman plus the evidence from the technical inspection. The likely cause provoked a long debate and the group also considered the timescale for getting back to normal train operations.

A Barnsley-based British Transport uniformed police constable arrived shortly after the accident. I asked him to control the onlookers, several of whom had arrived despite the remote location. Among those I authorised to be allowed on site was the local press reporter-cum-cameraman as this accident was newsworthy and I had to make sure the facts were presented properly. This very extrovert reporter did eventually turn up and proved most accommodating when asked to take specific photographs. He obligingly worked as the engineers requested and was rewarded with a very large streaky bacon sandwich and mug of strong, sweet tea in the breakdown van. The next day he very generously provided, free of charge, about forty photos.

To return to the accident, the early-arrived Mexborough shed master and his breakdown foreman quickly decided that two cranes were required, their own and the Gorton steam crane from the Manchester District. I knew the Mexborough shed master quite well as I had on several occasions met him at derailments in the company of my father. Understandably we got on exceptionally well during the re-railing process but, in truth, all the engineers worked excellently as a team in clearing up the mess.

Re-railing continued through the night and for some time during the next day. As the clearance work progressed, the civil and signal engineers made assessments of their requirements to undertake all the repair and replacement work. They had involved me in all the discussions so that I was able to keep Doncaster Control advised of the developing situation.

It was a continuous hive of activity which kept me constantly on the go. The saving grace was very strong, well-sugared tea which was constantly available, and the fact that the three fry-ups we had, of sausages, fat streaky bacon, eggs, black pudding, tomatoes, baked beans and fried bread, were worthy of Egon Ronay top star rating!

My relief, the local district inspector, up from his sick bed, arrived about 8.30a.m. on Day 2, and, after a comprehensive changeover discussion, *my 'first day' was finally over!* I retired to my lodgings at the pub in Silkstone very tired, very happy despite all the work and drama, and absolutely amazed at how this first day seemed to have gone. I was back on site by 6.30p.m. and worked with the district inspector until the line was open for train running. I must say I was very content then to get back to the more normal life of a station master.

I was allowed to attend the subsequent departmental enquiry which determined the cause of the accident as a fracture to the blade of the facing points. My father's sage overview of the whole event was simply that having done a difficult job it was the best thing that could have happened to me personally. Discounting the extensive damage and cost to the railway, I would have gained a great deal of valuable knowledge, experience and confidence. As usual, he was quite right. It was indeed a fortunately rare but truly valuable experience.

The Forth Bridge

Peter Caldwell's first experience of the Forth Bridge was as a young lad, but it was one he never forgot. Here he describes this and the train working over the bridge.

My father was a signalman, and he befriended an Edinburgh relief signal & telegraph man called Tommy. Part of the attraction was that they exchanged First World War experiences and, in addition, Tommy was a long-service man who had spent many years with the colours, some of them in India. In my dad's opinion Tommy was a signal fitter par excellence – every piece of equipment worked better after a visit from Tommy.

Unknown to me they cooked up a visit for me that every boy would dream about. I was just fourteen at the time, working as a train register boy in a signal box, and the war was on. Apparently I was to take the train to Dalmeny station on the south bank of the Forth estuary and meet up with Tommy who would be attending to the equipment in that area. However, one of the signals requiring Tommy's special tender loving care was on the bridge. You can imagine my excitement when Tommy announced that we would have to walk out onto the bridge to deal with this signal.

We set off from the end of the Dalmeny station platform and walked along the grass verge at the top of an increasing embankment with an end view of the bridge growing in size by the minute. The next thing I knew was that we were confronted and challenged by a group of soldiers with rifles at the ready. Tommy produced some sort of identification and, after a few jocular exchanges, we were allowed to proceed. By this time the embankment had given way to the stone arches on the landward side of the main cantilevers, and we were walking along a metal trough. Soon we were actually walking on the nearest cantilever, on a continuation of the metal walkway, until we reached the signal requiring Tommy's attention.

I can remember the experience as if it was yesterday. The weather was excellent, visibility wonderful, and the chasm below us was immense. There was the rumble of a freight train approaching, so Tommy and I moved into one of the recesses until the train had passed. When Tommy's job was finished, we had one last look around and then made our way back to solid ground. The soldiers waved and hailed us as we pushed on towards the station platform, there to join the train home.

What a day's outing; one never to be forgotten. However, that was not to be my last visit to that signal on the bridge. Years later, I crossed the bridge many times working trains to and from Fife, and on one occasion was stopped at that same signal.

One of the imperatives before working a freight train over the Forth Bridge at that time was the need for an examination, both by the C&W people and by operating staff, to ensure that all vehicles were fit to travel, that loads were secured thoroughly with chains and ropes, and that sheets were well tied down.

Traffic over the bridge was very heavy, and train paths were always at a premium. Before releasing freight trains to pass over, the signalmen at either end had to make sure that adequate margins were available to allow trains to reach the refuging loops at the other end, i.e. Dalmeny Junction or Inverkeithing, without delaying passenger services.

The approach to the bridge on the Dalmeny side is fairly level, but on the north side there is a heavy 1 in 70 gradient over about 3 miles, all the way up from Inverkeithing and through two tunnels to Forth Bridge North. To enable fully loaded freight trains to negotiate the incline, banking engines were a necessity. It was usual to have J35 bankers for this job, and they always assisted in the rear, working tender-first up the hill, so as to avoid having to pass through their own smoke in the two tunnels.

Trains to be assisted would sit in one of the loops at Inverkeithing, with the bankers in position. When a path up the hill was available, the signalman would start the process by clearing the appropriate signal. The leading engine would give a 'cockcrow' on its whistle, and the banker driver would open the regulator and thereafter acknowledge the 'cockcrow'. There would be an instantaneous explosion of power. The train engine would thunder through the loop crossing points onto the Down main line, then through the main line trailing crossover on to the Up main. The wagons would be jostling between being pulled and pushed. With the banker's regulator now in the big valve, the locomotive would be blasting with all its might, wheels slithering, the footplate shaking all over the place, and the firemen of both

A train of hopper wagons crosses the Forth Bridge. (Peter Caldwell)

engines shovelling coal into the fireboxes with all their strength. The bankers were never coupled to the train, so it was essential for them to keep up and maintain contact. Nearing the Forth Bridge, the banker would slowly ease off as the front of the train moved on to the flat approaches to the bridge, and the train engine would then take over the weight of the train.

The whole process was a good illustration of the efforts of men and machines involved in successfully overcoming the difficulty of working heavily loaded freight trains up steep gradients, especially on busy lines and with tunnels intervening.

Fish Supper

Nearly a hundred years after the building of Lowestoft's fish market Geoff Body had his first encounter with the railway involvement in the East Anglian Herring Season.

It was a cold early winter morning not long after the war and I was on my way to a first encounter with the East Anglian fishing fleet. The trawlers and drifters based at Yarmouth and Lowestoft had followed the other East Coast fishing vessels down from Fraserburgh and Peterhead, shadowing the great shoals of herring that were a favourite British dish. At the time I was still a lowly graded clerk with the old London & North Eastern Railway, quite new to the Norwich District and considering myself fortunate to have my period of summer relief work extended to this unfamiliar assignment. Quite apart from the pleasant anticipation of experiencing something new, getting any sort of relief job on the railway was a step up the long ladder of preferment and I was not immune from a small measure of pride in that fact.

My home was in Norwich, that marvellous city marriage of the ancient and the modern, and the approach to its Thorpe station never failed to impress me. From a position looking over the River Wensum towards the city it serves, the station has a great domed central section guarded by four tall chimney features and a clock pediment. Either side of this are two substantial wings with a *porte cochere* to complete the mixture of Renaissance and Classical styles. The building dates from 1886 when it relegated the former station to goods traffic use.

It was early. The concourse was busy but subdued, reflecting that peculiar commuter state of wakefulness without full engagement. The Lowestoft train was in No.5 Platform as usual. Services for the London, via March and via Dereham routes used Nos 1, 2 and 3 which consequently seemed to be the prestige side of the terminus. Quite logically the coastal services to Sheringham, Cromer, Yarmouth and Lowestoft used Platforms 4 and 5 but the latter always seemed the place for the most workaday trains and hand-me-down stock. And so it was today. The 'Claud' on the front looked slightly ashamed of its rake of coaches from every conceivable LNER constituent, several with clerestory roofs, some with the curious NER vertical panelling and tiny door handles, and with an overall roof line resembling the proverbial donkey's hind leg.

Despite the unprepossessing appearance of the train, at least some steam heat was getting through to the passengers wise enough to head for the front coaches. Lowestoft lay 23 miles 39 chains ahead and we would stop at nine stations on the way. The route was double track throughout, with six connecting junctions and two swing bridges, the Norwich-Reedham section of the line having been opened in 1844 and the section on to Lowestoft in 1847, both seen as part of a grand trunk route from the coast to the North. Along the senior section of the line my train followed the course of the River Yare, discharging quite a large number of its passengers for a day's work in Cantley sugar beet factory and then crossing the river over Reedham swing bridge.

The route now kept close company with the New Cut, owned by the railway and originally built to improve the coastal shipping access to Norwich and enable the city to avoid the high dues being charged by Yarmouth. Haddiscoe offered a connection with the main line to Yarmouth South Town via a swing bridge over the River Waveney which then became our own companion. By now the scenery on either side was flat marshland, nearly waterlogged and entirely empty save for the railway itself and the occasional windmill and pumping station. In the spring it would be filled with cattle brought in by rail for fattening on the rich marsh grasses.

Somerleyton swing bridge provided another example of these hybrid block posts which existed to control both rail and river traffic and to operate the mechanism for opening the bridge for the latter to pass. Junctions with the London line from Beccles and the Norfolk & Suffolk Joint Committee route from Yarmouth finally brought my train to Lowestoft Central.

A short walk along a road lined with ship repairers and chandlers led to a time-worn brick building, totally typical of countless railway goods offices around the country. In a room filled with standard tables and chairs, the latter worn by countless railway bottoms, I was given a place and joined the other clerks whose task was to produce waybills from the consignment notes for the fish forwardings. I could see that these were necessary to inform destination stations and to provide the basis for accounting and invoicing but it all seemed pretty unexciting. By lunch time I was bored stiff but consoled myself with a nice enough meal in the local canteen where white collar workers had a separate dining area and wooden chairs instead of the grim tubular steel ones of the main area. In later years I ate in the staff canteen at Somers Town Goods where stirring a cup of tea meant using a teaspoon chained to the serving counter!

Then it all went mad. I just had not realised that down at the fish dock vessels had constantly been steaming into harbour after their long sessions at sea. Even while I had slept the previous night the lumpers had been unloading fish, swinging the crans ashore for their contents to be boxed or to go for gutting, curing, smoking or some other process. An impressive sight as they approached the harbour entrance in all types of weather, the sturdy trawlers and drifters had continued to arrive, each registering its success or otherwise in the number of crans it had filled with fish, each cran holding 750–1,000 herrings and weighing nearly 4cwt.

Information about arrivals, quality and prices buzzed around the sales floor, orders were debated and agreed and soon cartage vehicles were heading fully loaded for the railway goods yard and the wagons waiting there to receive their contents. The result of all this activity was an absolute deluge of consignment notes being tossed onto the tables of our office. All of these had to be converted into waybills in time for despatch with the evening fish services, fast Class C vacuum-fitted freight trains which had top priority on their journey to London to ensure early delivery to Billingsgate fish market.

In the nineteenth century the pollution of the Thames had resulted in its fishing boats moving out to Harwich and other East Coast ports. Always needing extra business, the Great Eastern Railway was quick to provide tramway access to the docks at Yarmouth and Lowestoft and to improve the vans used for the carriage of fish. In the peak years just before the First World War, the annual landings of herring, mackerel and white fish at Lowestoft alone were around 100,000 tons and although this then declined steadily, despite the use of more modern steam trawlers, Lowestoft still had its own allocation of K3 locomotives for the daily fish trains to London until Class 40 diesels took over and the business finally petered out at the end of the 1950s.

Traditonal Lowestoft steam drifter.

It took a long time for my handwriting to recover from my time at Lowestoft but it was an unforgettable experience. In those days access to the crowded waterside area was not restricted by security considerations so that watching activities like the smoking of herrings and the 'beatster' girls making nets added immeasurably to understanding and being greatly impressed by the industry. A trawler making the transition from towering waves into the calm of the harbour, the noise and bustle of the fish sales, the cheerful and mildly lurid banter of the fishergirls who had followed the fleet south and bravely gutted ice-cold fish in ice-cold conditions, all indelible memories of my time at Lowestoft.

On most days someone in our office would cry 'Anyone for a fish supper?', nip out and purchase what had been ordered and bring it back in time for my homeward journey. It would be on my table for the evening meal, almost straight out of the sea and offering a taste so fresh that it would delight even the most demanding palate.

One False Move

Bill Parker was there when a simple, innocent action during the welcome for the Russian President nearly caused an international incident.

The early morning peak service had started at Euston station. Today, however, was a very special occasion and a number of things differed greatly from the usual. No.1 platform had been cordoned off. Quite a lot of passengers and other members of the public had accumulated behind the barriers manned by British Transport and the Met Police. The platform itself had been specially cleaned and the station had had a very strict security check. All those on the platform had been checked for weapons. The red carpet was laid. A fleet of limousines, including one of the Queen's Rolls, was lined up alongside Platform 1 in readiness for a motor cavalcade. Several station porters were standing by with trollies for the luggage. No one could doubt that something special was happening.

Platform 1 itself was somewhat crowded, with ministers from the Home and Foreign Offices, courtiers from the Palace, the Mayor of Camden and other civic dignitaries, and a number of policemen including the BT chief constable, senior officers from the Met and members of both forces. As the assistant district operating superintendent I was there along with my boss, operating superintendent Bill Haynes, several other district and divisional officers and our close colleague Bert Turner, the regional royal train coordinator. There were also huge-sized Russian security men galore.

The Euston station master was on the platform, resplendently dressed in top hat and tails, with the Russian ambassador alongside him. Everyone was waiting for the royal train. However, the Very Important Person coming was neither Her Majesty nor any member of the royal family. The train was carrying President Khrushchev, returning from Scotland during his state visit in the 1960s.

Apart from the exceptionally large number of 'guests and officials' and the various limousines, the arrangements were quite normal for the arrival of a royal train. People were in groups chatting away. I was with my boss, and the BT chief constable, the head of security at Scotland Yard and the Russian security chief, plus the district engineers of all the engineering disciplines – just in case!

The locomotive appeared into Platform 1. All eyes turned and closely watched the train slowly approach and stop precisely at the correct point, with the locomotive opposite the civil engineer's man holding a red flag. The double doors of the coach from which the President would alight were directly in front of the red carpet. The doors duly opened and the President, with a few bodyguards, appeared after several seconds. He was greeted by the station master, his ambassador, the UK ministers and the Mayor of Camden.

Everything was seemingly going perfectly when, suddenly, all hell was let loose. I and my group had a perfect view of what happened. Just a few yards away from us a very slightly built porter moved his hand towards the inside of his greatcoat. Within a split second, half a dozen of the huge Russian security men leapt forward and squashed the poor little porter face downwards onto the floor – and then sat on him. The speed and alacrity of the grossly sized Russians was absolutely amazing! Some BT and Met policemen then quickly formed a close circle round them!

The station master, the President and his small entourage, who had all seen the fracas, walked nonchalantly past the heap, which by then was emitting very loud noises, as if nothing had happened. It was not until the President was in the Rolls that the heap cleared and a very shaken and dishevelled porter, who was only reaching for a handkerchief from his inner jacket, was released.

Despite the incident being potentially serious, and one which might even have been a national disaster, I could not suppress a smile as the whole thing had all the elements of a Giles cartoon. I was not alone: Bill, commenting to the Russian security man and the senior police officers, in his inimitable manner with raised his eyebrows, eyes sparkling and with a small grin observed, 'It's all in a day's work'; to which I added, 'Happily, not very often in this country!'

Off the Beaten Track

Many a BR railwayman has contributed his time, effort and skills to the railway preservation activity, which has its full share of lively incidents as David Crathorn's recollections confirm.

Near Disaster

Back in the early 1960s I was working for the Caledonian Insurance Company in Birmingham and commuting daily from Wolverhampton by train. On my journeys I became friendly with a fellow traveller named David Plant, a trainee accountant. He was already a volunteer on the Welshpool & Llanfair Railway, which by then had been closed for normal operation for four years.

I began to go with David at weekends to work on the preservation of this former Cambrian Railways 2ft 6in-gauge line which ran for 5.5 miles from Welshpool to Sylfaen. We worked mainly on the track, clearing brushwood and young trees – but not digging up the turf as this was helping to hold the track together!

In early 1962 the managing director of the W&L, Fred Mayman, offered me the job of acting general manager for six months from 1 April. I agreed and arranged to leave my insurance job. The W&L wanted to have a representative on site at Llanfair Caereinion station, their intended headquarters. They needed someone who could help to use the volunteer labour to best effect, to recruit new members and to receive donations. Building good relations with the local community was also important.

I also had the benefit of a list from Colonel Robertson of the Railway Inspectorate detailing the requirements and recommendations to be dealt with before his next visit in the autumn for the pre-opening inspection.

As worksites stretched further from the base at Llanfair it became necessary to assemble in advance what was needed at the sites for the next weekend. Initially we would send out a works train with the small diesel locomotive *Raven*, but once we had received the Planet four-wheel diesel locomotive formerly on the Chattenden & Upnor line we had the option of hauling longer works trains, including dropping off wagons at more than one site.

On one fine day I was driving the Planet *Upnor Castle* from Llanfair with several wagons trailing behind the combination car. This bogie coach was our best vehicle, with a small brake compartment and other compartments originally intended for officers and ratings. My intention was to drop wagons at Cyfronydd station by shunting them into the loop. I was not too pleased to find that it was already full of stock.

I reviewed the situation and decided to move on, indicating my intention to the guard. The next mile is between fields, passing a level crossing where I slowed right down as there was no flagman. Fortunately the road was clear and I was able to carry on and accelerate for the 1 in 50 Dolarddyn bank which lay ahead. *Upnor Castle* took the train up the bank in fine style. As the gradient slackens the track curves left and then there is a level crossing protected by gates at Castle Caereinion. I had to stop short of the gate so I slowed down and put the loco brake on gently to keep the couplings taut.

Just as I thought we had stopped safely the Planet began to slip back, and I whistled for the guard's brake. I tried to halt the train with the loco brake, but realised that was no good. I hurriedly got out on the nearside and ran back to the combination car, putting on its brakes, but still the train was moving back. Increasingly desperate I ran on to the first four-wheel ex-W&L wagon and pinned down the brake there, but even that was not enough. On I ran to the second, similar wagon and was very relieved that when I put weight on the brake lever the backward movement finally ceased.

We very carefully secured the train and berthed the wagons in the loop at Castle Caereinion, a few at a time. An important lesson had been well and truly learned!

DIY Rerailing

In the early days of preservation on the Welshpool & Llanfair we had very few workshop assets. Indeed we had no workshop and our only pit was a stormwater culvert. But for the apprentices from Crewe works and other BR places we should have made very slow progress. We used to 'live off the land' to some extent and local tradespeople were very good to us. Stan Meredith, in the garage just up the street, readily helped us with metalwork and welding.

During one stay Stan mentioned to me that it had been a long time since he had ridden along the railway. The next time I planned to take the Planet out with some wagons I had no guard so I invited Stan to come along and told him what to do. We only went to the first station, Heniarth, where the original wagon loop was still there. I decided to push our wagons into the loop from the far end, as we planned to take a wagon from the Llanfair end back with us.

Stan joined me on the footplate for the shunt move and all went well until we were easing back out of the loop and nearly back on the main line. At this point the rear pair of locomotive wheels, which were leading, dropped off the track. The loco was on the switch at the time and not far from where it ought to be. What could we do? We had no tackle of any sort with us.

We cast about in the long grass and discovered two rail lengths and some half sleepers. A couple of these we placed across the track behind the loco. Then we inserted the shorter length of rail under the Planet's stout rear buffer beam and, using the sleepers as a fulcrum, put our combined weight onto the free end of the rail. With this improvised arrangement it proved surprisingly easy to lift the rear of the locomotive and swing it back onto the track.

We were rather pleased with ourselves as we made the journey back to Llanfair with one wagon in tow.

February Ice

When I left Llanfair Caereinion in autumn 1962, Mike Polglaze, nephew of Oliver Veltom the WR district superintendent at Shrewsbury, returned from East Africa to take over as general manager. I kept in touch and Mike asked me to relieve him so that he could go on holiday in February. He said that I need only go for a long weekend, as there was little going on during the week.

When I travelled up to Llanfair it was pretty snowy but we were not too delayed and arrived safely. The station was very cold and dismal. The few of us who were there discussed how best to occupy ourselves. Our 0-6-0T Beyer Peacock locomotive *The Earl* was in light steam and member John Boyle came up to me with the proposition that he should drive it to the water tower, a third of a mile away. John was one of those working on the locomotive and they were concerned that there was not much water left in the tanks. After another look at the weather, which seemed to have abated, I agreed to him going to the water tower, but no further on any account.

As time passed those of us at Llanfair station grew increasingly anxious when John did not return. Eventually we took to our cars, loaded bags of tools, and set off to find the missing locomotive. We found *The Earl* derailed at Cyfronydd station level crossing, well and truly blocking the roadway. The track flangeways had been filled with ice and the loco had simply climbed the rail where the track curves to the right.

We had only the locomotive's screw traversing jack, it was very cold and we were all pretty depressed by the situation. But, we set to work to inch the wheels back onto the rails. Like angels of mercy Mrs Millward and her daughter from Henllan Mill across the River Banwy turned up with trays of hot food and drink to cheer us up. Not quite so welcome was the man who came out of a bungalow just above the crossing to say that his wife was expecting and the ambulance would be there soon!

We knew we could never shift *The Earl* in time so we began to dig away the earth bank behind the loco and put sleepers down for the ambulance to cross the rails safely. We managed just in time. Not long after this we realised

The Vale of Rheidol single line from Aberystwyth to Devil's Bridge was, like the Welshpool & Llanfair, one of the small, narrow-gauge railways in main line ownership. Pictured here is its 2-6-4T, Swindon-built locomotive *Llewelyn*.

that the cold and our tiredness were slowing us down so much that we ought to secure the site, set red lights, and go to bed.

We made much better progress the next morning, aided by a member who had gone ahead to chip out the flangeways. But John Boyle did not appear much after that!

Waterside

Railway waterside links embraced harbours of every type from great docks to small coal staithes, and ships from cross-Channel packets to lake steamers and lowly ferries. Geoff Body describes some of his connections with waterside activities.

Getting involved with waterside rail traffic did not come until my time in London. There I was fortunate enough to be concerned with the vast activity of the docks on the north bank of the Thames in the decade before conventional wagon load movement to and from the huge rail network of the Port of London

Authority came to an end. Later, at Bristol, we had a little traffic from the ships in the city's floating harbour and a lot from Avonmouth, including many tons of bananas to move to ripening sheds at Spalding in vans provided with dry ice to keep the 'stems' and 'hands' cool and, hopefully, to see off any nasty tropical spiders which had taken an involuntary trip to Britain. The Bristol division even had its own 'fleet', admittedly only the three diminutive vessels working the ferry service between Kingswear and Dartmouth.

In London I had some understanding of the dock labour situation and its problems but the reality came to me in quite an accidental way. An important flow of traffic for us was the movement of imported hides to Morland's factory at Glastonbury in Somerset. Transport was the responsibility of a shipping firm in the City and I made frequent trips to their semi-basement office to ensure we retained the business and to make the practical arrangements. They were a nice bunch and when we disagreed about the maximum load we ought to be getting into a wagon the very sensible outcome was to go down when the next shipload came in – to Victoria Docks, I think – and view the problem on the spot.

In due course the visit was made and I watched the stiff, shaped carcasses come off the vessels for loading into wagons. The dockers handling them were a good bunch and, without malice, suggested I tried to load one myself. A sensible idea which could not be rejected without shame! In no time at all I was encased in a heavy, incredibly awkward, unbelievably smelly, totally dark and unforgivingly stiff cavern which resisted any attempt to manoeuvre it. Walking over the edge of the quay would have been just as likely as finding the wagon door, although I did manage the latter with a few good-humoured and highly facetious directions from the assembled onlookers. Between us we did find a method of improving the number of carcasses we could get into a wagon but the smell from my experience of real dock labour remained with me all the way home that night and prompted some unflattering reactions from fellow commuters and my family.

I had a very soft spot for our Poplar Dock which had grown from an early timber pond off Blackwall Reach and had its own sufferance wharf. Several of the pre-grouping railways had depots within this North London Railway waterside enterprise but the Luftwaffe nearly ended its existence in September 1940 when much of the depot was burned down and nearly 200 loads of damage debris had to be cleared from the site. In my time it was still very active under the control of Jim Burnham and then Fred Pullin, both admirable railwaymen. Until the LMR and ER parts were merged there was some interesting rivalry between them and between their respective lighterage agents, Union Lighterage for the former and Vokins for us. The latter were a delightful company with very gentlemanly directors but totally skilled in the business of transferring goods from shipside to dock and not easily bested in the practicalities of carrying it out. Further competition was provided by the Western Region's Brentford Dock until that was closed.

By the time I moved to Freightliners the whole port and shipping worlds had changed. Containers were the answer to rising handling costs and my depots at Cardiff and Southampton were very much involved. Pengam depot at Cardiff dealt with a large amount of fruit imported by the Citrus Marketing Board of Israel as well as steelwork to Newport docks. At Southampton our Millbrook terminal was soon to get a neighbour in the highly mechanised Maritime terminal, built while I was area manager but owing much to terminal manager Dick Scarley and his deputy Jack Wickens. The ship to tug and trailer to crane movement was very sophisticated but very few hitches occurred either in building the vast new terminal or in running it.

I did have a near miss with a personal hitch, though. I got on well with the Dart Line's Captain Peter Doble who kindly arranged for me to be

Poplar South Dock: A row of barges are moored beside the cranes at East Quay with the coal hoist beyond.

Very traditional operations at Poplar Dock in 1963. Bags of starch are being unloaded from ship to railway wagon.

Above: The Freightliner Maritime terminal at Southampton with shipping in the background and both train and transfer trailers beneath the massive overhead crane.

Right: With dockside cranes towering above, citrus fruit is being loaded from warehouse to Freightliner container at Cardiff.

shown over one of his new container ships. The actual tour was fascinating, surprising me with just how many of the shipboard activities and movements were automated. My helpful guide and I saw hardly anyone as we roamed around the vast areas below the main deck.

Sailing time was 2.00p.m. but at 1.45 it slowly dawned on me that my companion was lost and, in growing desperation, had resorted to trying every companionway to regain daylight. There was no one about to guide us and until the very last moment I was convinced that I should have to call my wife on a ship to shore facility to say that I was delayed, and was there anything she wanted me to bring back from the United States!

All in a Life's Work

In the course of his career Alex Bryce held a wide variety of positions, all of which contributed to his rich collection of assorted memories.

Is Your Journey Really Necessary?

My railway career began on 23 February 1942 when I reported for duty as a junior clerk in the booking office at Kirkintilloch near Glasgow. The female clerk on duty, Ruth Scott, was busily engaged in issuing tickets for passengers, mainly anglers, travelling on the 8.05a.m. branch line train to Aberfoyle. As most of them bought their day returns to Balfron at 3s 3d a time, Ruth was clearly enjoying showing me her great skills with small printed card tickets being dated on the old-style dating machine, whisking them out of the rack and in and out of the clumsy iron dating device in one fluid movement. However, as time drew near for the train an older and rather impatient gentleman demanded a day return to Buchlyvie for which, alas, there was no printed ticket. Issuing this would have involved consulting the pre-war fares book, increasing this figure by war time percentage increases, writing out and dating a blank ticket and recording it in the blank card register.

Keen to avoid this exercise, Ruth emphasised to the passenger that everybody was going to Balfron that morning, but he angrily stressed that he was going to Buchlyvie, whereupon she retorted that the fishing was apparently very good at Balfron. This clearly enraged the passenger who demanded he should be issued with a Buchlyvie ticket without any further fuss. Ruth pointedly enquired of me whether I could hear the steam-hauled train approaching the station and when I confirmed it was she brusquely instructed the passenger to pay for his journey at the other end!

As he anxiously dashed off over the footbridge to join the arriving train Ruth remarked to me that this was the first lesson I must learn – that there is always an awkward customer! At this time outside each ticket window was a permanent poster 'Is Your Journey Really Necessary?'

Not in the List of Duties

As an assistant district operating superintendent at Burntisland in the 1950s one of my key tasks was to make surprise visits to level crossings and signal boxes to ensure all was in order and all regulations were being carried out. Around one lunchtime in the St Andrews area I made such a visit to Leuchars Junction signal box where, after signing and examining the train register, I enquired of the resident signalman about the unauthorised presence of a young man sitting in the corner of the box near one of the windows. The signalman informed me that he was the signalman from one of the lesser

The ready-use rack for card tickets, an early version of which is shown here, remained largely unaltered for over a hundred years. (*Illustrated London News*)

wayside signal boxes and in his own time he came to the Junction signal box to study the working and develop his experience and career prospects.

This impressed me greatly but when I went over to the young man to converse I was astonished to find he had clearly been having his hair cut, and the evidence was there that my untimely visit had interrupted this operation. It was necessary for me to 'read the Riot Act', leaving both men in no doubt that they were guilty of a very serious offence which could endanger safe working, and it would be necessary for me to advise their station master accordingly for appropriate disciplinary action.

The older resident signalman was deeply apologetic and insisted that he was really the one who should take the blame and the younger man should not suffer as a result of it. As my father had been a signalman at one time I had some sneaking sympathy for the older signalman's concerns about his having been caught in such an outrageous situation, but as I descended the stairs from the signal box I was astounded when he called to enquire of me whether he could complete cutting the other half of the young man's hair!

Last Man Standing

The introduction of Freightliner services to the East Coast Division of the Scottish Region in the early 1960s involved setting up a new freight sales organisation and the appointment of eight new freight salesmen. My boss at that time, the divisional commercial manager, had recently returned from BR's Woking Senior Management Course and was anxious to carry out the search and selection of the very best candidates using the most professional procedures. We succeeded in finding over forty appropriate applicants and the DCM directed we would see the majority of them during an intensive week of interviews to be held, for effect, in the main boardroom at the Waterloo Place, Edinburgh divisional HQ offices.

As the new divisional sales manager I arranged with my secretary for the individual candidates to be directed to the boardroom on my personal telephone call to her so as to make sure we were ready for the next interview. We were seeing seven applicants a day in a very intensive, and indeed tiring, series of interviews involving each candidate assuming the DCM and I were senior executives of a major potential Freightliner customer. The candidate would be invited in a selling exercise to promote the benefits of the new Freightliner system.

At the end of the third day of this process I invited the secretary to send in the final candidate but was surprised when the door to the boardroom opened and a head wearing a flat cap nervously appeared with a rather haunted look! He was invited to join us after removing his cap, raincoat and scarf and on completing this it was very clear he appeared to be much older than we could have wished.

However, we did not wish to reject any candidate out of hand and, after he was seated at the boardroom table, the DCM hesitantly enquired as to why he was seeking to be one of our new freight salesmen. A glazed look came over the candidate's eyes as he responded that he was not sure about that as he understood from his boss, the goods agent, that he was to be presented that day with a tea-making appliance in recognition of his long service within the industry!

The DCM, perhaps a little lacking in a sense of humour, was very put out that such an error in our arrangements should have happened. But after explaining where our system had gone wrong and perhaps too readily seeing the funny side of it, I was astonished when my colleague responded by reminding me that we might actually have appointed the man!

The Green Lady

As a relief station master in the 1950s I was engaged one November to cover the station master's post at Arrochar & Tarbet station on the West Highland Line, owing to the sudden illness of the resident station master. It was necessary for me to obtain lodgings during my stay and there was initial difficulty in finding a suitable place at rather short notice.

The staff on duty on my arrival comprised a signalman and a porter who were ultimately able to find me lodgings in Arrochar House, a very old and very significant building with a long history as the former residence of a notable 'Laird of the Manor'. Among the locals it had a reputation of being haunted by a 'Green Lady' who apparently had an illicit love affair with one of the servants and was murdered by her husband the laird. She continued to remain and haunt Arrochar House and had allegedly been seen by many local people.

As we waited for the last train of the day, the staff regaled me with various lurid stories of the activities of the Green Lady and when I left the station to walk in complete darkness the half mile to Arrochar House I found myself dwelling a little nervously on how I would get on in my new lodgings.

The route took me off the main road and onto a side road leading to the gates of Arrochar House and as I walked I was suddenly conscious of an eerie sound coming along the road towards me. It seemed to be the sound of a chain being dragged along the ground. As it directly approached me I became increasingly uneasy and indeed broke out in a cold sweat. In the darkness there was nothing to be seen, and the sound appeared to go right through me and continue along the road in the opposite direction.

The headlights of a car from the direction of Arrochar House shone along the road and as I looked in the direction of the receding noise I witnessed a Collie sheepdog padding along the road trailing its chain behind it! I was greatly relieved that I had not encountered the Green Lady although my ninety-year-old landlady assured me she was regularly seen around the area, but thankfully not during my two weeks stay.

False Evidence

As a relief station master at Fort William my duties involved working at the various stations between Crianlarich and Mallaig, on the West Highland Line, virtually all of which had a resident station master. The man in charge at Glenfinnan was Patrick Monaghan who had a legendary reputation for being in constant trouble with head office in Glasgow on similar lines to the escapades of the former cinema celebrity Will Hay.

Monaghan bred top-class racing greyhounds which won many major awards at the famous Scottish Greyhound stadium at Powderhall Edinburgh and head office staff, including senior officers, looked forward to the reliable tips Monaghan could convey on potential winners.

Monaghan's greyhounds were allowed the run of Glenfinnan station and could often be found in the ticket office or on the platforms. On one occasion, when a military train was passing to Arisaig and a single line token had been withdrawn for handing to the driver, one of the greyhounds snatched the pouch from the instrument and set off along the railway line. It was hotly pursued by Monaghan who finally retrieved the token but unfortunately the military train was delayed for over 15 minutes and Monaghan knew he would be in big trouble with head office and in particular with the formidable West Highland district inspector Lachlan McKinnon.

The inspector reported that he would be coming on the next train for an urgent enquiry with Monaghan about this unacceptable delay. The latter, realising he would be on a serious disciplinary charge, decided that special action was necessary. Accordingly he went to the local stables, filled two buckets with manure and then walked along the line to a point where he removed staples from the trackside fence to provide proof of his hastily contrived excuse that the delay to the train arose from cattle trespassing onto the railway. This, he planned to say, had made it necessary for him to leave the station and take appropriate action to clear the line.

On the inspector's arrival at the station Monaghan insisted they should walk along the line to verify the evidence of the broken fence where the cattle had come onto the track. He had scattered the horse manure there and pressed Lachlan McKinnon to understand what a great job he had done in clearing the line for the safe passage of the military train.

They returned together to the station with Monaghan soliciting and expecting praise for his efforts. Instead he got a resounding rebuke, the inspector saying that as a country lad he certainly knew the difference between horse sh–t and bull sh–t!

The Prince and the Plants

Planning for the movement of the Royal Train and its faultless arrival at the destination station on the occasion of official royal visits was one of the more challenging and, indeed, sometimes more stressful experiences for railway operators.

As assistant district operating superintendent Burntisland I was deeply involved in a royal visit to Tillicoultry in the late 1950s and worked closely with my opposite number in the civil engineer's department. An important feature in planning the arrangements involved the overnight stabling of the train in a suitable secure and secluded siding outside the station and its subsequent arrival at the station at the appointed time.

Another important (perhaps even critical!) exercise in planning the arrangements was the setting down of the red carpet on the platform at the precise point where the Queen and the royal party would leave the train. This operation was a joint one involving the assistant DOS and the assistant engineer and it required very careful measuring which took into account the exit doorway of the train plan and the point where the locomotive would bring the train to a stop on the arrival at the station.

It was normally an anxious moment for those concerned as the train slowly arrived at the platform and moved very carefully towards the forward stopping signal, especially as there were many VIPs present in the welcoming party.

Tillicoultry station had been freshly painted and refurbished with very generous help from a local paper-making company who were to be visited by the royal party to mark the company's centenary anniversary. They had decorated the station with lavish floral displays including a number of exotic tropical plants placed closely together along the sides of the red carpet.

As the train arrived on time and slowly and nervously proceeded towards the stopping point, it finally came to a halt almost exactly where it should be but unfortunately a few inches beyond the precise point where the exit doorway of the train was aligned with the red carpet. The royal equerry was first to leave the train and, realising the leaves of the tropical plants might get in the way of the Queen, he carefully held them back so as to avoid any contact with Her Majesty.

Unfortunately as Prince Philip followed closely behind the Queen some of the leaves of the exotic plants brushed against him and our station master, as one of the main reception party, overheard the irritated Prince remark, 'Watch out for the bloody camels!' The visit went off well with no other incident.

The Gesture

The era of Doctor Richard Beeching and his highly controversial closure of uneconomic railway branch lines was a very difficult and emotional period in railway history which seriously strained relationships between central government and, in particular, voters in Scotland where many lines and stations were closed down as result of the policy.

The proposed closure of a branch line was attended by a very stringent and legalistic procedure involving a comprehensive investigation by a special branch lines closure team which took into account various users' sensitivities and forward projections of any possible changes in passenger and traffic flows that might justify the line being reprieved and retained for future prospects. Dr Beeching, however, was not much in favour of the 'jam tomorrow' argument.

There were many well-supported legal objections and in such cases the closure proposals would be considered by specially convened tribunals with all aspects of the plan being subjected to rigorous arguments involving highly qualified legal teams. The voluminous statistics submitted with the closure proposals and the assumptions made were vigorously challenged and the arguments brought forward to support withdrawing services had to become increasingly innovative and convincing.

For example, during the preparation of the supporting evidence for closing the celebrated Royal Deeside Line between Aberdeen and Ballater (for Balmoral) it was submitted by BR that, based on the then actual passenger use of the line and the level of its current operational deficit, it would be cheaper to pay for a taxi for each regular passenger and offer him or her a 10s note towards personal expenses. There was abundant evidence that many of those most vocal in the arguments against closure in these deeply rural areas made virtually no regular use of the services for their own journeys!

As assistant district operating superintendent Burntisland during these difficult times I had reason to be on duty in the control office for the passage of a special train conveying the chairman, Dr Beeching, from Edinburgh to Aberdeen. We received the train on time from Edinburgh and conveyed it safely and punctually through our district, handing it over to our Aberdeen colleagues on time at the boundary point Kinnaber Junction.

My opposite number in the Aberdeen district control subsequently telephoned me to report that the train arrived on time at Aberdeen and the chairman remarked that he was very impressed by the morale of the Scottish railwaymen along the route. Apparently many of them had exchanged the 'Victory' sign with him as his train had passed!

Colonel G.W. Parkin
BSc, C.Eng, FIEE

Alan Sourbut reminisces about a notable character he worked for, pictured below in a photograph provided by his son.

Geoff Parkin was the electrical engineer in charge of Stonebridge Park Electric Depot in the late 1950s until it closed in the mid-1960s. I worked for him at several places and was greatly impressed by his professional ability and highly individual character.

His early days were in Blackpool and Merseyside, and, despite his being expelled, so he said, from Blackpool Grammar School, he attended university after being in the Royal Navy in the First World War, which he told me he joined under-age by giving a false birth date. Between the two world wars he became engineering superintendent on the unique Mersey Railway and in his free time held a civilian pilot's licence.

In the Second World War he rose to the rank of a REME colonel attached to the 42nd Division of the East Lancashire Regiment. In Africa he was taken a prisoner of war, but escaped from the POW camp in Italy and trekked over the snow-covered Appenines to freedom when he met the Eighth Army moving north.

G.W. Parkin was a brilliant engineer, forthright and blunt in manner both with his staff and higher authority, and never losing his Lancastrian accent. He had a sharp mind and admired hard-working staff but had little patience with those with lesser qualities.

My first experience of GWP was in the early 1950s when he was engineering superintendent of the Mersey Railway. This outfit was taken under the wing of the electric traction engineer for Merseyside, R.C. 'Jumbo' Smith. As a senior draughtsman in the Liverpool office, I saw the interaction between Parkin and Jumbo, both of whom were very strong characters. From being a large fish in a small pool GWP had become a small fish in a larger pool. That situation could not continue for long, and GWP was moved to London Midland Region HQ at Derby as electrical assistant to the chief mechanical & electrical engineer.

The role GWP played at Derby did not last long either as main line electrification was looming. Alec Emerson, from the Eastern Region, was appointed electrification engineer with responsibilities both for the existing electrification and for the new 25kv projects. GWP had to go! He accepted the vacancy for electrical engineer in charge of Stonebridge Park Electric Depot on the understanding that he could choose where to live, and chose Brede village near Hastings, but living in digs in Wembley during the week until his retirement. I was his assistant at Stonebridge Park for several years.

Stonebridge Park power station supplied power for the Euston–Watford and Broad Street–Richmond electric train services. Although his responsibilities also covered Euston station, the Euston House offices and St Pancras station, along with Stonebridge Park main rolling stock workshops and the sheds at Willesden and Croxley Green, GWP gave the greatest part of his attention to the run-down power station. He would visit the complex out of office hours, talking to staff of all grades and unearthing information on the bad practices and plant problems, a process which duly led to frank confrontations the next day!

The main plant at the power station consisted of two 20,000kw turbo alternators. The peak load in winter was of the order of 24,000kw, easily covered by the two sets, but during April–September the load fell to some 17–18,000kw, enabling one set to be stripped and overhauled each summer. It was always a tight programme, made worse towards the end of one summer when a fitter owned up to losing a nut in the turbine. The plant had to be dismantled to retrieve the errant nut, but with much overtime and sweat the job was completed in time. All this and much work on ageing and badly maintained plant gave GWP great scope for implementing new techniques and making other improvements at the station.

Situated within the Stonebridge Park complex was a laundry, unique for an engineering depot and probably throughout the railway network. It was quite large and had the capacity to cope with the complete servicing – washing, ironing, repairing etc. – of all the linen from the large rolling stock depot at Willesden, from the passenger vehicles, sleepers and dining cars. It was also responsible for meeting the laundry requirements of several BT hotels and of other BR rolling stock depots in the London area. The laundry had its separate management and supervisory structure, but GWP had the overall responsibility vested in him and he carried it out impeccably.

GWP had a dotted line responsibility to the Euston district operating superintendent; and had a superb rapport with those incumbents over the years. This was most evident at their regular review meetings which were always conducted in a courteous but positive, effective and cooperative manner. The operators often commented about the engineer's competence and professional attitude; and that he could always be relied upon 'to deliver the goods satisfactorily and on time'. However, at least one young assistant district operating superintendent was rather apprehensive in GWP's volatile presence, fearful of saying the wrong thing and provoking the inevitable sharp reaction!

An incident typical of this able and very distinctive character involved the two chimneys of Stonebridge Park power station which were the highest in the neighbourhood. After completing a job of pointing repairs on one chimney, the steeplejack supervisor on the job presented GWP with his men's work sheets, adding, 'I don't suppose you will want to check the work.' Predictably GWP took up the implicit challenge and climbed right to the top of the chimney with no equipment other than the ladders! This was the nature of the man. He was unafraid of people, of work or, indeed, of any situation, however dangerous.

Something of a rebel with a great respect for practical matters and people, Geoff Parkin never had much regard for Derby HQ and, not a man to disguise this, often sent critical letters there. Following one extreme example, the regional engineer travelled from Derby to the depot to command GWP to take the letter back and promise never to repeat such a missive. GWP had to accept this but made it clear to his senior staff that he was pleased with 'having made Derby sit up and take notice!'

GWP's interviewing techniques were also somewhat unusual. It was not unknown for him to discover a weakness in a candidate's technical understanding and then produce a reference book and sit alongside the astonished person and give him a lecture on the subject. His desire was that people should understand engineering principles in order to become better engineers.

Staff problems and consultations were normally delegated to the senior engineers, but GWP had a great keenness to improve safety standards. Each year he would hold a safety meeting with all the staff representatives – fifteen or sixteen in total – in his very large office. He put a lot of time into preparation for these meetings and was even known to arrange for someone to provide tea, coffee and biscuits, at that time something never tried before.

The lads were most helpful, after all they were having an easier day and there were some safety issues well worth discussing. However, one of the representatives, a turner in the main workshop, was always suspicious of anything he thought management was up to. He was an excellent worker and a qualified first aid man who normally worked his lathe with his head uncovered, but on receiving a call from his boss's office would promptly don his cap. This upset GWP but he put up with it in the interests of good management – staff relations. When those attending the meeting were asked whether they preferred tea or coffee, this particular representative, cap still on, would retort ungraciously, 'Neither.' Watching this scenario I used to have the distinct feeling that first aid might be needed for GWP's heart attack!

As one of G.W. Parkin's Liverpool office people and one whom he disliked initially, I went on to become his assistant for three years and slowly gained his friendship and support. I saw him as an abrupt man, forthright in speech whatever the situation or company, brave in behaviour and beliefs and full of respect for staff who were loyal and competent. He never bragged, he was a fantastic engineer and an unforgettable character who totally gained my respect and support.

Signal Box Coming Up, Sir!

Peter Rayner remembers another colonel.

I went to Leicester in the early 1960s, a sales representative with a Mini, to visit key customers in the area from Sharnbrook to Oadby. We sales reps all had Minis, except Cyril Bleasdale who had a Jaguar. Managers then had Ford Cortinas but Cyril was always different! Among the local station masters and goods agents were John Edmonds at Kettering and Jim O'Brien at Market Harborough. Both were destined for high places and to overtake me in rising to the highest echelons of the BRB. John went on to be chief executive of Railtrack.

Anyway, Jim, John, Cyril and I had Colonel Gardiner as our divisional manager, a man feared by some and loved by others, but handled carefully by everyone. It is of Colonel Gardiner that I tell. Firstly there was the case of John Edmonds who, keen to demonstrate his cutting edge even in those days, had his cartage costs displayed on the office wall. The colonel, instead of being pleased, tore a strip off John for defacing the walls!

I had to present myself and my car on a Saturday morning for inspection, not on sales results but on the cleanliness of the car and our turnout. It is easy to laugh at these army-style traditions within the railway service but we were, after all, a uniformed, hierarchical structure and I, for one, was proud of that life. Later, for example, when I was more senior, I treated my chief inspectors with respect, and they me with a formality that belied the affection beneath.

So, why 'Signal box coming up, sir'? Well, Colonel Gardiner was before his time in some respects. In the '60s it was not forbidden to take a drink; forbidden to be drunk, of course, but it was still a sensibly balanced society

Controlling signals called for very varied housing, from small ground frames to large conventional signal boxes. Some had to be located wherever room could be found.

without the modern 'over the top' attitudes. I am still involved in work and consultancy and nowadays would not dream of taking alcohol during the working day.

But back then much was different. On the inspection tours in the saloon there was drink for the officers and their guests. However, Colonel Gardiner felt, perhaps correctly, that the staff outside should not see us taking drink. So, poor John McAvoy, the divisional operating superintendent, was charged with the task of announcing when a signal box was due so that we could hide our drinks under the saloon table. Along we went on the branch lines with their mechanical signal boxes to the accompaniment of John shouting, oft times wrongly, 'Signal box coming up, Sir!' Then, 'Signal box passed, Sir!' And so it went on.

John himself had served as an officer under Colonel Gardiner during the war and it is said that when the divisional manager telephoned him in his office John always stood to answer the call!

Farm Removal

Basil Tellwright was ready and eager for the challenge of his new job but nothing had prepared him for the first project that confronted him.

I was appointed to High Wycombe Western Region as the freight sales representative in January 1963. My duties were to maintain and expand the local rail freight activities jointly with the goods agents at Maidenhead, High Wycombe and Princes Risborough, and to develop the substantial paper and associated traffic in the Woburn Valley.

On my first morning the High Wycombe goods agent greeted me with the news that he had heard from a Mr Donald, a farmer located some 5 miles east of the station, who was interested in moving his farm in its entirety to Newton Abbot. By this period the once-extensive rail business of moving whole firms, farms, factories and the like was little more than a memory and the goods agent admitted that he had never handled anything like a farm removal. He was not too happy when I had to confess that I knew even less than he did.

For want of a better idea we went to check on the state of the facilities in the full load yard. It had a cattle dock and associated pens in a very rundown state, but was well equipped with mobile cranes which dealt with the containers of furniture traffic from the local industries. The yard foreman also had never handled a farm removal, but typical of his kind, he refused to let any traffic problem get the better of him and was quite delighted with the idea of tackling one. The mood was infectious and we felt ready to visit the farmer.

When we met Mr Donald it was clear that the wellbeing of his cattle was paramount. He did not want them 'crammed into a cattle lorry over that distance', as he put it. I was already uneasily aware that farms were complex places with animals that had minds of their own and equipment of peculiar shape, size and variety, and what we saw did nothing to alter that feeling. The move would involve not only forty head of cattle, two tractors and every conceivable type of farm machinery but also the contents of the farmhouse, two cars, the farmer, his wife and their dairy assistant. Taking our courage in both hands we made positive noises and arranged for a divisional loading inspector to make a visit to check that everything could be loaded and moved safely and within gauge.

At this time BR still had a number of SCVs, Special Cattle Vans, built pre-war to move prize animals to and from shows. They had separate stalls for up to eight animals and a central compartment for an attendant. One was ordered for Mr Donald to see and when it arrived I went down to the yard and was amazed to find that the yard staff had scrubbed the vehicle out and polished every bit of metalwork. Not only that, but the cattle dock itself had been cleaned and painted and the surrounding area weeded and spruced up. Mr Donald was equally impressed and a price was agreed for the move to take place after the summer harvesting.

My initial anxieties were beginning to subside. More vans arrived and the staff, pleased to be doing something out of the ordinary, cleaned and polished them in turn. Mr Donald, on his own initiative, began to bring down some of the equipment early and also asked us to move thirty tons of hay in addition to the items already agreed. Fortunately one of the older members of the yard staff remembered how this should be loaded. Pickfords quoted to load the furniture in two BD containers, a cattle float was arranged to ferry the cows down to the yard after milking, and the delivery arrangements were laid on at the other end.

On the day of the movement, apart from the late arrival of Pickfords, everything went exceptionally well. As batches of cows were milked, Mrs Donald saw them into the cattle lorry for transfer to the yard and by 18.00 all were down at High Wycombe. The foreman told me afterwards that the farmer knew each of his animals by name and sorted them so that 'friends' travelled together. The milking parlour was cleaned and by 19.00 I had brought Mrs Donald and the all-important milking machine down to the goods yard. The train, including the passenger coach with blankets for those travelling in it, could now be put together.

At 19.30, dead on time, the farm removal train pulled out of the yard to the cheers and goods wishes of the many friends who had arrived to bid the Donald's farewell. I had the settlement cheque in my pocket and when we established that the arrival and delivery at the Newton Abbot end had also gone well we could at last relax and savour the fact that we had been part of the last but one farm removal ever to take place on BR.

Thorpe Marsh Coal Trial

Bryan Stone brings to life a day spent with a block train load of coal, a dynamometer car and an attempt by worn-out Austerity 2-8-0 No.90005 to cope with an extra 61 tons.

In September 1964 my 'day's work' was to learn, as thoroughly and systematically as possible, the tasks of management and staff of the then Doncaster division. My rigorous programme did not really allow for the divisional freight inspector's friendly call: 'Can you be on the Colchester (i.e. early morning, 05.01 from Doncaster) and come with me on a dynamometer car load trial with Thorpe Marsh coal?' Such invitations were, however, too good to miss, so on 7 September 1964 we met, warmed up at Retford (district inspectors always knew where to find a mug of something good), caught the 06.28 diesel multiple unit to Worksop and set off on foot to the train in Worksop yards. It consisted of twenty-three big 24.5-ton loaded hoppers, unbraked, and a 20-ton brake van. A normal block load was twenty-one hoppers at 750 tons. This load was rated as eighty-one 'Wagon Units' with a calculated weight of 811 tons, including the dynamometer car.

Many railways were built to carry coal and it was their major business and revenue provider. This coal train on the LNER was a commonplace scene.

The dynamometer car was behind the engine, with an expert team from Derby on an errand which would turn out quite differently to their usual jobs, which involved flitting up the main line behind new diesels at high speeds, and then going for dinner in the Station Hotel. Today they would just once, for a few seconds, touch 22mph. Looking bashful at having had greatness thrust upon her was 2-8-0 Austerity locomotive No.90005, with a Retford crew who obviously had their own misgivings about being the 07.47 special from Worksop to Thorpe Marsh. So let me take you back with them, and me, into a part of the railway network which even many professionals never got to see, and for an unusual day's work in the one-time Yorkshire coalfield.

In the 1960s the big new coal-fired power stations in South Yorkshire burned a lot of coal. Today's job went to Thorpe Marsh, just north of Doncaster, on the old Great Central/Hull & Barnsley joint line, already closed north of the power station. Thorpe Marsh coal came mainly from South Yorkshire and North Nottinghamshire, collected in Worksop, but was variously selected and blended, so the block trains and empty returns often ran as specials.

The pits' output in this region, bordered roughly by the East Coast Main Line, the GC main line, and the Don Valley, seems today unbelievable. Silverwood Colliery, for example, in the 1990s had beaten all records to produce 1 million tons in a year, but others ran it close. Silverwood we will meet again, as it was on a minerals tramway, once called John Brown's Railway, which connected Silverwood, on its hill, to the Sheffield–Doncaster line of the Great Central in the valley floor, just west of Mexborough at Thrybergh Junction. From Silverwood Siding, 1.5 miles dropped at 1 in 47 in a vicious S-curve. Remember, our coal trains had no automatic or continuous brakes, and some spectacular wrecks had gone into history there.

Coal going to Thorpe Marsh ran first to Braithwell, then turned left and, at Silverwood, wagon brakes were pinned down for a precipitous helter-skelter down to Thrybergh, to then continue more sedately along the 'main line' through Mexborough. It then took the Doncaster avoiding line to Sprotborough to regain the GC/H&B. Today the pits are closed and the track mostly lifted but it was then quite busy.

I had toured this district quite a lot, 'observing the working', as management trainees should, riding in brake vans and on Austerity 2-8-0s. The Austerities were the general-purpose coal and steel traffic workhorses of the Doncaster division; we still had some sixty by this time. There were also the O4s of GC parentage, already fifty years old, many built in and for the First World War, but they mostly covered heavy trips and pilot jobs.

The Austerities had been built for the War Department in 1943-45, hence the official class 'WD', 935 of them, raw 2-8-0s based crudely upon Stanier's LMS 8F. Designed with a minimum of resources, they were, like other military material, intended, if not destroyed, to be dumped when finished with. After military service on the Continent that good idea had been forgotten; most came back, often in poor condition. In 1946/47 the LNER bought 200 of the best at £4,500 each, and BR later took another 533 at about £2,700 each. One of the LNER's first lot was No.77046, built by North British in May 1943 for £11,400, which became in due course LNER No.3005, and in 1964 was BR No.90005 at Retford shed.

These engines, although uncomfortable and unloved, worked hard all over Britain, but by 7 September 1964, No.90005, twenty-one years old, was much the worse for wear, filthy, leaking, and with worn tires and flanges, weak springing, knocking and banging, and with many detailed defects which would now never be repaired. Her driver was well aware of the situation. She would, in fact, be condemned only seven months later. But today she was coupled and wired up to the test car for measurements and speech transmission.

I was invited to ride in the car with the Derby specialists. Having studied physics and engineering, this was very tempting. Remember there were no computers or calculators; all measurements were recorded mechanically, though accurately, by spring balances and steel pens on paper rolls, and most calculations were made by slide rule. But the day would show that some of the academic refinements would scarcely be required. No.90005 was to reveal her unusual gifts, and they were not what the plan had laid down!

The original Austerity specification had been to handle 1,000 tons at 40mph. The design had two large outside cylinders and a boiler pressure of 225lb/sq. in. This gave a tractive effort, i.e. pull at the coupling, in theory, of 34,215lb. The precision belies the crude calculation, because it could vary considerably according to wear, and No.90005 was worn out. Achieving 40mph was a vain hope. But worse was in store. Austerities were notorious for slipping, as adhesive weight on the driving wheels was too little for their tractive power. Slipping was always accentuated by badly worn wheel treads, as well as bad track and damp rails. All of these were present today, together with all the usual unmistakable Austerity sound effects, which the enthusiasts called the 'ring of the motion'.

We left Worksop Yard at 07.58 with one quarter regulator and pressure showing at 190lb. Uphill at 1 in 150, No.90005 was already slipping, and 'lifting the water', i.e. priming. The 3 miles to Brancliffe East took 12 minutes, clattering downhill through Shireoaks station at 22mph, the fastest we went all day. Stopped at Brancliffe's 'home' signal for 3 minutes, before taking the branch, we now faced serious trouble. From the junction the line climbed at 1 in 100. Full cutoff, one quarter regulator and 190lb on the gauge, had us barely moving, slipping continuously, and, at 1.5 to 2mph (faithfully recorded in the dynamometer car), producing extraordinary tractive effort readings of between 30,000 and 42,000lb. No wonder she slipped! Just 23 minutes after leaving Brancliffe East we slipped to a noisy stand near milepost ¾. The driver gave us a 'thumbs down'. It was going to be a long day!

'Slipping to a stand' would, for Austerity experts, only produce a tired yawn; but No.90005 was now standing on catch points, designed to protect the main line junction behind us by derailing any inadvertent backwards movement! The driver was duly anxious, the whole train stretched out with taut couplings. The guard's brake was applied, rear end wagon brakes pinned down, and the catch point lever held safe. No.90005 was then allowed to roll gingerly backwards to leave twenty-one units, a quarter of the train, and the brake van, on the grade and try again. It took 13 minutes to cover the next quarter mile, accelerating triumphantly to 3.5mph. The summit at MP2 was passed at 11mph, and we rolled down to Dinnington where the load was made up out of the colliery yard, again to eighty-one units. A pilot engine must have rescued those we left behind, for we did not go back.

Now on the Mid/GC/H&B joint section, we set off to Thurcroft, the 2.5 miles taking 10 minutes, where we stopped again. From here to Silverwood only one line of the double track was now in use, and single line working was by staff and ticket. Leaving at 09.37, the 3 undulating miles to Braithwell took 16 minutes. At Braithwell, where the direct old route, now out of use, stretched out straight ahead, the fireman caught the ticket for Silverwood on the fly at 7mph. We turned left onto the Midland/HB branch to Silverwood, stopping there at 10.14, 12 miles and 2 hours 15 minutes from Worksop. The driver gave up the ticket, reflecting on his misfortunes. From here, not moving, but stopping, was to be the next challenge!

The guard, inspector and myself pinned down brakes along the whole train. This was a handwork skill where you dropped the big brake lever from its catch, leaned on a brake stick for leverage, and slipped the pin into a suitable hole in the bracket to retain the brake lever. What effect this had, unless you inadvertently blocked the wheels, was impossible to tell, but if you did them all, it was usually erring on the safe side.

It is even today widely known that Austerity engine brakes were poor, with many a runaway recorded in their day, and there was no reason to suppose that No.90005 was any exception; rather the opposite. We had 811 tons behind the engine, on 1 in 47, 60 tons over the rated full load. We were very, very careful. A problem is, however, that when the brakes are pinned hard down, the train must then be pulled into motion again. No.90005 tried. Slipping and spitting, she came after a few seconds to another helpless stand. It is tempting at this point to let off a hand brake or two to help to get rolling, but very dangerous, because you will need them again very soon. A train once out of control stayed out of control.

Walking or standing alongside the engine, with a little ash ballast on the firing shovel, slid carefully under the leading drivers and, of course, extracting the shovel quickly enough, is an age-old trick which helps against slipping, and at 10.26 we tried again, measuring momentarily 42,000lb tractive effort while pulling against the blocked train before it started to move. Then, as

No.90005 and each wagon reached the brink of the 1 in 47 gradient, gravity took over. The 1.5 miles down through the S curve to the bottom at Don Bridge East took 15 steadily clanking and squealing minutes, the section time given in the working timetable.

We stood at signals at Don Bridge for 30 minutes, picking up the pinned brakes, another act of skill and brute force, and now they were hot. We had to await a path on the busy main line from Rotherham to Mexborough. Once out and over the junctions at Thrybergh, a steady tramp at 13–15mph then took us to Mexborough station, where we stopped again. An Austerity tender held 5,000 gallons of water, and we had come but 19 miles, but the constant slipping had emptied boiler and tank alarmingly. Spending 12 minutes taking water in the station platform ensured our popularity there, expressed in good Yorkshire terms!

We set off again, now on a good road, partly falling, to Cadeby and off up the Doncaster Avoiding Line to Sprotborough Junction, passing through the crossover onto the H&B without stopping at 12mph. From there, the rest was easy. Another 4 miles, partly coasting, had us at Bullcroft Junction at 12.25 where No.90005 and the test car were detached to turn on the triangle, and re-attached behind to bring the coal to the stop board at the power station. It was now 13.02, 5 hours from leaving Worksop. We had covered 27 miles but it had all been a close-run thing.

Coal train running in these districts was notoriously erratic. Long waits, incidents and mistakes could cost hours. On 13 August, three weeks before, on the footplate of No.90522 on a Thorpe Marsh block load with 750 tons, I had left Worksop at 11.37 and not reached Thorpe Marsh until 17.52. On that occasion 3 hours were spent idle at Thurcroft because the single line train staff had been left at Silverwood Junction for an Up (southbound) train of empties, running 3.5 hours late. Someone knew, but no one had asked. Add to this the increasing unpredictability of the engines, and efficiency was obtained only with a struggle. Failures on the road were also commonplace by this stage. I have a note from the Doncaster control log of 1 September 1964, from Frodingham shed, that of forty-five allocated steam locomotives (at this stage almost all heavy freight engines) twenty-one were at start of work under or awaiting repair, and two more Austerities failed during the morning. Yet Frodingham, at Scunthorpe, served one of the greatest single sources of Eastern Region freight income.

On my present trip we eventually returned from Thorpe Marsh to Bullcroft, while our new friends in the dynamometer car wondered how they were going to get back home with their valuable equipment. They had come from Derby, with booked special workings, and still had to get back to Worksop, and then Sheffield and Derby. My sandwiches were long gone, but they had the catering well organised. Lunch was served. Eventually, back at Bullcroft, my inspector friend and I had had enough of trials, coal and Austerities, and so took our leave, walking up to the nearest road to wait for a Corporation bus back to Doncaster, only 5 miles away. It had been a long day, and we were tired and filthy. At least

No.90005 with a dynamometer car and the trial coal train at Bullcroft Junction. (Bryan Stone)

we didn't have to work back with the engine! It was a two-edged grace, the 'romance' of steam in those last years.

What was it all for? Two more wagons on each train, 49 tons of coal, would have been money in the bank, but it was asking too much. I often wondered whether No.90005 was really the best they could do at Retford shed that morning, but the shed would close a year later. No.90005 was laid aside in April. The other steam engines would go too, spares and proper repairs were non-existent, and nothing was likely to work well for long. No.90005 was in a parlous state, and as I referred to boiler pressures you may have noted that these were far below the boiler's rated 225lb/sq. in. In fact, we never saw a pressure above 190lb. Yet the tremendous (if momentary) tractive effort readings showed a different story. Perhaps the gauge read 15 per cent too low, but that too was strictly a reason to refuse to take her out on the road. No, all was not well. What the staff thought of their standard block load, behind their flagging Austerities, being increased in future by 60 tons was not discussed. It was perhaps as well.

What happened next I never found out. According to my notebook, here on a Swiss office desk forty-six years later, I was next morning riding on No.61087 on the 05.49 Doncaster to Cleethorpes, for another study project. And the railway we thought we knew, and of which this had been part, was fast coming to an end. I am glad now that I was in time to see it.

The 246 Ladies of Kings Cross

It takes a lot to surprise lifelong railwaymen. They have come across most situations before. However, for Bill Parker there was one exception.

It started at my first London Transport Users Consultative Committee meeting, during the second week into my tenure as divisional manager at

Kings Cross. After my piece explaining what I intended to do to improve punctuality, frequency and reliability of the suburban services I thought that I had done fairly well, particularly as some of the other London divisional managers had been given quite an 'active' time. Maybe, I thought, it was because I was a new boy, or because it was getting very near to lunchtime.

I was, however, rather taken aback when, from the other end of the table, came a question from a very small lady whom I could hardly see. 'Mr Parker, what are you going to do about the ladies of London town at Kings Cross?' My immediate thoughts were that the lady was either an expert on Noel Coward's songs or that she was referring to the Shire ladies who I knew were complaining about the poor state of the toilets at Kings Cross (and, more emphatically, about the fact that they, and not the men, had to pay!). Before I could reply, although I really could not think of a constructive reaction, she followed with, 'All those prostitutes from the North on Away-Day tickets; from Leeds, Newcastle and Durham.'

Glancing round the table I noticed that, not surprisingly, some of the men were grinning. I chose a standard MP's reply that I would *personally deal with the matter*. Stung by the reference to Durham I added the throw-away, and totally irrelevant, line that, 'My wife comes from Durham.' By this time the other men at the meeting were thoroughly enjoying the exchange and wished me lots of luck, among other things!

I enjoyed the joke from the chairman after the meeting when he privately assured me, in deadpan fashion that, 'Prostitutes at London stations would not be pursued by the TUCC…(*hesitation*)… on its agendas!'

My first job back at the office was, nonetheless, to find out from the BT police superintendent the exact situation at Kings Cross. I did know, having worked at several London and provincial stations on the railway network, that railway stations were favourite and remunerative touting places for prostitutes. The superintendent quickly and quite nonchalantly gave me a rundown of the current situation, on the law, the fact that he had 246 'ladies' on his records and that, in a couple of weeks time, the BT and Met police would move them on to Paddington and then, eventually, in an anti-clockwise direction round to the other London terminii. He offered me a tour of Kings Cross to give me an insight into the situation when I next stayed in London, which he duly did and which I found most enlightening!

I decided to leave the matter primarily to the police as I was informed by my area manager and office staff that there had not been any complaints from the public, passengers or staff. And so it remained for five years, apart from the occasional enquiry of the BT police superintendent at our regular liaison meetings.

That is, until it was mentioned at my retirement presentation. There, at the end of the speeches, a voice was heard from the back of the hall, that of my long-standing professional friend Major Peter Olver, Inspecting Officer

Rather different 'Ladies of Kings Cross'. A contrived line-up of HSTs at Kings Cross produced the picture given by the area manager and staff to chairman Sir Peter Parker on his retirement. (Charles Wort)

of Railways at the Department of Transport. He recounted how he had received, via the Health & Safety Executive, a formal complaint from Post Office staff, who leased part of Wellers Court, that prostitutes were occupying the premises actively, and read the reply from the regional general manager's office to the effect that 'Mr Parker was off sick in bed with a bad back but that he would *personally deal* with the prostitutes on his return to work.' Unsurprisingly this generated considerable laughter.

Peter Olver was immediately followed by deputy general manager Colin Driver presenting me with a guard's watch inscribed 'From the ladies of Kings Cross – we never had it so good.' The hilarity and humorous and dubious comments that followed do not require much imagination. One, which I understand continued well after my retirement was, 'Is there any wonder that the Kings Cross area always hit its income budget with such potential sources of "fee" income so close at hand?'

There was, unfortunately, one exception to the fun, happily only for a short time. My very good friend and well-respected missionary of the Kings Cross Mission, of which I was the active president, went very red-faced with embarrassment at the idea that his president might have been associated with the trade. However, all was quickly explained and forgiven(!) and we continued to be good friends.

Things were then made worse a little later when, at a subsequent retirement party at York and in the presence of the senior managers of the region and their wives, the same ladies purportedly sent a bouquet of flowers which was again presented by Colin Driver. This time the accompanying card was inscribed 'We have still never had it so good!' It was a blessing the missionary was not present!

I suppose there still are, and perhaps always will be, Ladies of Kings Cross.

Writing this prompted Bill Parker to recall an earlier and more personal incident at Kings Cross.

I also recall a small brush with the law in Kings Cross station in my serious courting days back in the mid-1950s. As a district inspector I had an alternate week on-call responsibility with the district inspector covering the former Great Central line to Calvert (excluding Claydon LNE Junction), and this meant me lodging in London during the on-call weeks.

My wife-to-be came to London once or twice during those weeks when we had 'high tea' and went to a West End show or classical concert. She went home to Welwyn Garden City on a late theatre and concert-goers train. We said our goodbyes in the darkened doorway of the Grade 2 listed German Gymnasium near the suburban station.

One very cold winter evening, to our utter astonishment, we were accosted by a BT policeman and told to move on! On making a simple query as to why – since we were not misbehaving in any way and certainly not speaking or acting in a provocative manner – he told us firmly that 'he was not having any prostitutes on his patch', and repeated more positively that we should 'clear off'. Highly embarrassed, we moved off at top speed into the suburban station.

A good job there was no arrest or our forthcoming marriage might have been blighted and my wife might not have become first lady of the Kings Cross division twenty-three years later!

Missing Persons

Hugh Jenkins, a most able railwayman and certainly not careless, did however manage to lose two people.

Missing Minister

I will never forget the day Transport Minister John Moore was placed in our custody and we lost him at Crewe station. He was on a ministerial tour of inspection and it was considered he needed a posse of minders which included myself, BRB vice chairman David Kirby and regional operations manager Peter Rayner.

Arriving on one of the platforms the minister announced that he was going to the Gents and disappeared into one of the caverns that passed for such at Crewe. Knowing the boundaries of their supervisory role, his minders dutifully stood back and waited outside. Ten minutes passed and the minister had still not emerged. Pursuing him inside seemed unseemly and so the waiting group hung on for another 10 minutes, fully expecting to see their charge emerge, slightly embarrassed, into the sunlight.

Then, suddenly, across three platforms, our quarry was spotted, busy conducting a solo inspection of the parcels operation there. We had forgotten that the Gents had two entrances and will never know whether the minister had got lost inside and mistaken his exit or cleverly given us the slip.

Find Albert

The other loss involved the very pleasant and obliging Stoke division chauffeur Albert Lakin who was universally addressed as Albert. On one occasion divisional operating officer Harry Potts and I were in Aberystwyth to finalise arrangements for chairman Sir Peter Parker's visit to the Cambrian Coast Line and to check the facilities for the formal dinner he was giving for local people of influence. When we saw the room booked for the event it turned out to be in the hotel basement, without natural light and smelling of stale tobacco. We said nothing to the hotel manager but decided to start early the following day to search for something better.

Albert was staying in a different hotel. This was an odd sort of social convention but probably suited everyone. However, we needed to advise him of our planned earlier start. It was about 11.00p.m. and the front door of the small hotel was locked and the lights out. Banging finally attracted the proprietor's attention and convinced him that we needed to contact Albert. 'Albert who?' he asked, not unreasonably, but we had forgotten our chauffeur's surname. After all nobody ever used it.

The combined efforts of Harry and myself managed to come up with a description which the proprietor seemed to recognise. Off he went up the creaky stairs and, after what seemed like an age, reappeared with a bemused man in dressing gown and carpet slippers. Unfortunately, it was not Albert.

Thankfully we did find the real Albert and the next day made a dinner booking at a more suitable venue. The chairman's tour was a great success despite the confusion of the previous evening.

On the Central Wales Line

In 1948, needing a house for himself and his wife, Dennis Simmonds successfully applied for the post of station master/goods agent at Llanbister Road, also in charge of Llangunllo.

A line of summits, curves and spectacular scenery, the Central Wales Line from Shrewsbury and Craven Arms to Llanelli and Swansea was born of

This guard's handlamp typified the universal use of oil lamps on trains and for illumination at the many smaller and more remote railway locations.

the LNWR's push to link up with the line from Llanelli to Llandovery and access the coal and mineral business of the Swansea area. At one time through trains from Euston conveyed people to the spas of Llandrindod Wells and Llanwrtyd, but essentially the line was a remote rural outpost, important to its area, but quite difficult to work.

The station house was not immediately available when I took up my new post on 8 November 1948. Arriving at midday, I introduced myself to the porter, Harvey Morris, who gave me a brief introduction to the station, pointed out the house where I was to lodge, then put on his coat. Surprised, I asked if he was going for his meal-break but he told me he had finished for the day, and that I was on the late-turn by myself!

I went to the house indicated and was met by Mrs Palfrey, an octogenarian widow who lived there with her brother Percy. He was a coalman, employed by the Radnorshire Company, and worked alternate days at Llanbister Road and at Llandrindod Wells. For the latter, which considered itself rather 'posh', he was punctilious in having a wash on the preceding evening.

The rest of my first day was spent familiarising myself with the layout, and meeting the signalman on duty. All of the lighting was by oil lamps, and those on the platforms had to be lit by using a taper with an oil handlamp. The station was 848ft above sea level and in a valley, and subject to heavy winds, which made lighting a difficult task. On many occasions the taper and the hand-lamp flame would be blown out making it necessary to take the heavy lamp cases from their posts into the waiting room, then carry them back after lighting.

Percy returned from Llandrindod Wells on the last train, introduced himself, and told me that the meal at my new 'digs' would be ready very shortly. Having put out the lights and secured the station, I followed his trail, and found that Mrs Palfrey's ideas of cuisine were very similar to some I had met in the army! Worse was to follow when, the following morning, I met my predecessor Mr Lloyd emerging from the door of <u>my</u> station house. I learnt that he had transferred to Penybont, two stations down the line, where there was no station house to move to!

Between Knighton and Llanbister Road the Central Wales Line passed over Knucklas Viaduct, through the 645ft Llangunllo Tunnel and over the summit to Llangunllo station before the long, curving section to Llanbister

SIGNAL BOX COMING UP, SIR!

Road. Freight trains were assisted in both directions as far as Llangunllo with a banking engine in the rear from Knighton and a pilot engine on the front from Builth Road. Guards were involved in careful brake work to keep wagon couplings tight.

The formation was single line, with a passing place at Llangunllo, the sections either side being worked by electric train staff released by holding down the commutator key to allow a staff to be withdrawn. The section staff had to be replaced in the appropriate instrument before another could be withdrawn so that the train driver in possession of the staff had an absolute guarantee that the section ahead was clear. The staff itself was of cast iron and some 2ft long and needed skilled handling on the part of the fireman to exchange staffs while the train was moving. The most important point was for the fireman and the signalman each to concentrate on the staff he was receiving, leaving the recipient to ensure he caught the one being delivered.

Passenger traffic was light and, at Llanbister Road, generally concentrated on daily journeys to and from Llandrindod Wells for employment or education, and to Knighton on Thursdays for the weekly market. My first Thursday evening was memorable. Being unfamiliar with the temperament of the locals, I did not appreciate that they would always finish a conversation before alighting from their train. On this occasion the last Down train was running late and, having shouted 'Llanbister Road' a couple of times with no sign of doors opening, I gave the guard 'Right Away'. A few minutes later, the signalman came to tell me that several of our passengers had been carried on to Dolau, the next station. Fortunately, there was a return train (the last of the day) 20 minutes later; there was little delay in opening the doors when they got back! The different attitudes of the passengers, some of whom had looked on the beer when it was brown, was educational. One was threatening to report me to Abergavenny (which housed no one in my chain of command anyway!), while another embraced me, telling me that I had been a good friend to him.

Those travelling to school on the 08.30 train both received and provided education. It was noticed that the train was often checked at the home signal at some stations, and it was found that a young couple from our area were pleasuring each other in the leading compartment and the various signalmen were taking the opportunity to view the proceedings. Apparently the other passengers were leaving the compartment for the lovers' sole use, so that they could walk past to the toilet and witness the spectacle!

There was a goods shed at Llanbister Road, where grain and fertiliser traffic was stored for collection by farmers. The Radnorshire Company also had a coal stacking site, Percy unloading the wagons and the foreman (Dick Jones) dealing with customers. The principal activity came on Thursdays, when cattle and/or sheep were loaded for transport to the market at Knighton. For the autumn ewe and lamb sales we would forward as many as 1,500 sheep.

There was a cattle dock in the yard which accommodated two wagons, and the remainder had to be loaded using a moveable ramp. Sheep are reluctant to lead the way but will usually follow one another, and so it was necessary to grab one by the fleece and drag it up the ramp, when the rest would follow. As Harvey Morris was approaching retirement age, and his stamina was below average following exposure to mustard gas during the First World War, this task was usually my responsibility.

The sheep-loading process was complicated by the fact that some farmers would bring dogs with them. Had they been sheepdogs this could have been helpful, but some were cattle dogs, which barked and confused the sheep. Occasionally, one sheep would break away and run along the cutting. True to their nature, several others would follow, and Herculean efforts were necessary to round them up and also to ensure that the remaining flock did not follow.

Unsold animals were returned on a night freight train, in the small hours. The wagons were marshalled next to the locomotive, usually in screw-coupled, vacuum-braked wagons, and uncoupling them was complicated. The train was standing on a 1 in 80 falling gradient, and so the couplings were compressed and impossible to unscrew. It was necessary to pin down brakes on subsequent wagons, drop the front part forward gently so that the couplings were loose, detach behind the cattle wagons and then propel them into the siding.

Prior to my arrival, there had been a serious collision at Llanbister Road. The single line approached on a 1 in 90 rising gradient, which changed to a 1 in 80 falling gradient at the station. Freight trains carried a red tail-light and two side-lights which showed a white light to front and rear. One night, the signalman was walking up the signal box steps, having collected the train staff from the fireman, when he realised that he could not see the brake side-lights and assumed that the train had become divided. Contravening the regulations, he replaced the starting signal to danger. The front portion came to a stand and, in due course, the fireman came to the box to establish the cause and the guard arrived to confirm the position of the rear portion. The front portion was set back onto the single-line, re-coupled and went on its way without further incident.

Some months later, another signalman experienced similar circumstances and, building on his knowledge of the previous incident, dropped back the starting signal, and the front portion came to a stand. THEN ... he saw the side-lights, as the rear portion crested the summit and raced down the falling gradient until it collided with the stationary front portion, causing an obstruction which closed the line for several days.

In 1949 I think, possibly 1950, an inspection of Sugar Loaf Tunnel was undertaken on a Sunday. One of the staff saw a loose brick in the roof, tapped it with a hammer, and it fell out. It was decided to station an observer in the tunnel (not an enviable task) to report on any adverse reaction. Some days later he heard rubble falling onto the roof of wagons as a freight train passed. He promptly raced to the end of the tunnel and put down detonators to stop the next train. These exploded efficiently, but the train continued at speed through the tunnel. The line was then closed and, some days later, the entire ventilation shaft collapsed. For some months freight trains were diverted and passengers were conveyed between Cynghordy and Llanwrtyd Wells by bus.

On 1 January 1949, the Central Wales Line was transferred from the London Midland Region to the Western Region. Later that month I was visited by the auditor, who was perturbed to find that I had been entering check marks in green pencil which, on the LMR, was the normal colour. Auditors used a blue pencil, the use of which was prohibited for all other staff. On the WR, the colours were reversed and I had to mend my ways! Another aspect which caused him a problem was the purchase of milk for the goods shed cat which kept us rodent-free. Because our freight cash revenue was small and infrequent, this was bought with passenger cash, and the receipt was cleared through the coaching account. However, he considered this to be unacceptable, and required that I raised the debit on the freight account, then prepared a transfer credit voucher to the coaching account!

A few weeks later we had a visit from the legendary Gilbert Matthews, superintendent of the line. He was accompanied by Mr Storey, the acting district traffic superintendent from Swansea Victoria, who was so well briefed that he had to ask the district signalmen's inspector what my name was!

Following a change in regional boundaries, staff were given the option of remaining with the Western Region or returning to the London Midland. If the latter was chosen, two vacancies would be offered in the applicant's own grade and, if both were refused, the individual became a member of Western Region staff by default. As there was no chance of my getting the station house at Llanbister Road, I opted to return to the LMR and, mid-1950, I was offered the post of station master/goods agent at Peplow, a station on the line from Wellington to Nantwich which had recently been transferred from WR to LMR but was still controlled by the WR district traffic manager at Chester, Norman Briant.

Once bitten, twice shy, so I rang to confirm the status of the station house, and was told that the former occupant had transferred to Crudgington, where the station house was empty, and he would move there as soon as a bathroom had been installed. So I confirmed that I would like the job at Peplow. Norman Briant was incandescent that the post had been offered to me without his approval but, as it was offered under the option arrangements, the only way he could prevent the appointment would be to prove me unsuitable, so he called me to his office and gave me a stiff 2-hour examination on Rules & Regulations. Happily I had recently passed my annual examination and had no problems.

Circus Trains

Civil engineer Jim Dorward took a special interest in circus trains, not only writing about them here and elsewhere, but also modelling circus and rail vehicles for his garden railway.

During the 1950s and early 1960s Britain's three main circuses all used rail to a greater or lesser extent. Bertram Mills, the top-quality show, used four trains, three of them for circus trailers and the fourth for animals. The Mills' equipment and operational practices were copied from Knie in Switzerland and Ringling Brothers and Barnum and Bailey in the USA but, of course, BR's relatively restrictive loading gauge had a considerable influence on the design of their trailers.

Billy Smart's Circus and Chipperfield's Circus only used rail for the transportation of animals and consequently the Bertram Mills' movements were the most interesting and challenging from the BR viewpoint. Starting and finishing the seasonal tour at the Mills' winter quarters at Ascot, the circus trains not only carried the big top and its paraphernalia on bogie flat wagons but also the executive caravans, the trailers for administrative, costume and other functions, the generators, blacksmith's forge, catering items and the equipment of all the other support activities of this major entertainment enterprise. Passenger coaches were provided for the erection and dismantling staff.

The routing of the trains was often quite complicated. For instance, three of the trains had to arrive at the destination station with the drawbars of the circus trailers facing the end loading bank. This sometimes required the trains to take a circuitous route which might involve reversals and the movement of the fitted head from one end of the train to the other. Although these trains were mainly restricted to 25mph this did not normally cause difficulty for BR as the journeys were made during the night. However, the storage of the long Mills' trains was often a problem, usually solved by working them to a suitable yard, which might be some distance away.

A circular issued by the district traffic superintendent at Hull details the arrangements for a movement of Bertram Mills Circus which took place after the Saturday show at Hull on 19 May 1962 with arrival at Scarborough early the following morning. The first trailer train left Hull Paragon at 10.30p.m. and, like the 1.30a.m. and 3.30a.m. departures, ran via Hessle Road and Cottingham South to turn so that the circus vehicle drawbars would be the right way round for unloading on arrival at Scarborough Gallows Close. At Hessle Road the local pilot engine from Paragon came off and a second pilot removed the rear brake van so that the train engine, K3 2-6-0 No.61906

TUESDAY, 31st JULY AND WEDNESDAY, 1st AUGUST.
HUNTLY TO ELGIN.
Bertram Mills Circus.

Headcode	2Z	2Z	2Z	2Z
Reporting No.	296	297	298	299
	(Tues.)	(Wed.)	(Wed.)	(Wed.)
	pm	am	am	am
Huntly ....dep	10 30	1 30	3 25	4 30
Cairnie Jn	10 51	1 51	3 46	4 44
Keith Jn ....arr	11 7	2 7	4 2	4 54
Do. dep	11 10	2 10	4 5	4 55
Mulben	11 25	2 25	4 20	5 5
Orbliston Jn	11 45	2 45	4 40	5 18
Elgin West ..arr	12 5a	3 5	5 0	5 30

Loading of Trains.
No. 296. Conveys SK, GUV, 6 Bobols, BV.
No. 297. Conveys SK, 10 Bobols, BV.
No. 298. Conveys SK, 9 Bobols, BV.
No. 299. Conveys 3 SK, SCV, 9 HBs, 3 CCT, BG.

Speed of Trains.
Nos. 296, 297 and 298. Speed must not exceed 25 miles per hour.
No. 299. Speed must not exceed 35 miles per hour.

In the event of it being necessary to detach any vehicles en route due to defect or other cause, the Guard must advise Bertram Mills' representative travelling on train.

Details of the train arrangements for a move of Bertram Mills Circus from Huntly to Elgin. The SK coaches are for the circus staff, the Bobol flat wagons for the large equipment and the GUV and CCT covered vehicles for the animals. (Jim Dorward)

for the first train, reporting number 2Z15, could leave on its journey without delay. The third train, departing at 3.15a.m., took the circus staff and animals direct to Londesborough Road, Scarborough, and was allowed a maximum speed of 30mph.

The main designer of the Mills Circus movements was Cyril Mills, one of Bertram Mills' sons. On one memorable occasion the BR inspector in charge of the shunting refused to follow the printed instructions resulting in the build-up of the circus being seriously delayed. The inspector thought he had a better idea. Not surprisingly Cyril Mills made his views on the matter very clear. Fortunately the circus staff managed to recover some of the lost time with the result that, later in the day, Cyril was able to be in his place for the arrival of the Town Mayor for the opening of the first performance. Mr Mills opened the car door and who should step out wearing the mayoral chain of office? Yes, the same BR inspector.

An Unusual Royal Train

Royal train journeys were traditionally planned down to the last detail and well in advance but Don Love found himself faced with a much less structured occasion.

By 1984 I had been area manager at Liverpool Street for four years and knew the funny ways of the Great Eastern which thought of itself as the poor relation of the Eastern Region with its grand HQ at York. I was regarded as a foreigner from over the water (i.e. the Thames), having come from the Southern Region. Our Division was the natural successor to the GER but had just been abolished as part of the many reorganisations, leaving York headquarters as the next level of management.

My area included the line from Hackney to North Woolwich which was slowly decaying until the GLC put some money into it, but the major breakthrough came when the LDDC was set up to develop Docklands. Suddenly money was available and the curator of the Passmore Edwards Museum asked me to help set up a new museum in the restored North Woolwich station dedicated to the Great Eastern and the thousands of railwaymen who had lived and worked in and around Stratford over the years.

I gave him open access to anything he wanted from the Great Eastern and loaned him a retiring relief station master to search for suitable items. Some were still being used – but in the museum they went! They managed to furnish a replica 1920s ticket office from tickets to pen nibs, all of the GE/LNER period. In the end the museum contained anything from silver cricket trophies from Stratford Market to GER furniture, some from my office! Mervyn Rogers at Southend was in charge of the drivers at Stratford depot and produced the punishment book from Stratford loco depot which recorded cases of drivers being fined for using too much coal, together with an Eastern Counties Railway chair. The Great Eastern Hotel at Liverpool Street came up with a complete GER table setting.

At one of the meetings the curator said he could arrange for HM Queen Elizabeth, the Queen Mother, although by now eighty-four and not accepting engagements beyond six months ahead, to open the museum and wouldn't it be nice to have a steam-hauled royal train from Stratford. I agreed.

When I got back to the office Keith Watson, my operations manager, clearly thought I was mad but was happy to help. York HQ was of the same mind but would have nothing to do with it. Keith remembers that I instructed him not to go through official channels laid down for the operation of steam locomotives on BR. The popularity of Her Majesty in East London coupled with the opposition of headquarters guaranteed cooperation from everyone on the Great Eastern!

The *Flying Scotsman*, owned by the Hon. Bill McAlpine, was available and could be worked down from Carnforth hauling an excursion train. Despite an ASLEF strike only two weeks before, Mervyn and his train crew assistant Keith Ion found a number of drivers at Stratford were willing and able to drive and fire the locomotive. Carriages of a suitable quality were located at Bounds Green.

I had been involved in arranging royal trains before and meetings were held with the police, engineering and other interests. No chances could be taken! There was no engine release at North Woolwich so the royal had to be followed by another locomotive and hand signalled. The *Great Eastern* diesel was polished up for the occasion.

The North Woolwich terminus in 1967, 120 years after the impressive Italianate building was constructed on what was then riverside marshland.

By this time the Mayor of Newham was involved and a tea party had been arranged for HMQM in a marquee to be erected at North Woolwich. But there was still a fundamental problem, one which had bugged me from the start. Was the locomotive within gauge for the North Woolwich branch? All the older railwaymen said they had worked there before. I could find no 'engine restriction' book, so we had to find out the hard way!

Flying Scotsman had arrived at Stratford a couple of days before the opening day, 20 November 1984, and was polished up and stood gleaming to the admiration of the commuters. We decided to run it the day before the royal in order to 'feel' its way to North Woolwich with Mervyn, the district engineer Paul Leach, and his bridge engineer, on board.

A minor derailment occurred at Liverpool Street that afternoon just before the evening peak which meant that Keith could not be on the *Flying Scotsman* – not a good omen – but with such a gathering of management talent on board and the GE locomotive standing by, I had no worries! The first hurdle was the long bridge under the GE main lines. The bridge engineer stood on the running plate with a torch – he knew the clearances were tight. The chimney missed by inches but steam cleaned the underside of the bridge and the soot and muck of ages fell back onto the engine. The locomotive subsequently cleared everything until approaching North Woolwich when it touched a piece of angle iron on the underside of a closed overbridge. Later in the day, the angle iron on the offending bridge was cut away and we were all clear!

On the big day itself all went well. I appointed myself officer in charge of the train, Paul Novac was station manager Stratford and Ben Elliot, ASM Liverpool Street, assumed the role of station manager North Woolwich. I had to turn down a request for Her Majesty to travel on the footplate!

A cheering crowd at North Woolwich greeted Her Majesty where she met the crew, and we proceeded to the marquee where she formally opened the museum and said what a great pleasure it was to travel behind this historic loco, 'As I did with my husband many times on our journeys to Scotland.'

All went perfectly, and when everyone had gone and I had changed out of my top hat and tails, a few of us adjourned to a pub opposite the museum for a well-earned pint.

After twenty-five years the museum closed for lack of funding and its collection was dispersed to York National Railway Museum and the Great Eastern Railway Society. 'York' had its way, after all!

Fenland Tales

Despite its featureless landscape and simple, straight railways, Jan Glasscock found that an assistant area manager's life in the Fens was not without incident.

A Novel Expedient

On one occasion the last wagon of a train of vanfits loaded with sugar beet pulp from the BSC factory at Ely became derailed between Black Bank and Manea on the fenland route to March. It bounced along at the rear of the train for some 3 miles before becoming uncoupled, the parting of the vacuum pipe bringing the errant wagon and the rest of the train to a stand. Fortunately the Up line had not been obstructed but some 3 miles of track was damaged on the Down, including that over the Welney Wash bridges.

A freight train was used to examine the line with the Up line being pronounced clear by myself, as the assistant area manager, and usable for single line working. I was subsequently 'rapped over the knuckles' for passing it as safe before a civil engineer had examined it but pointed out that clearly only the completely separate Down line was damaged and a reasonable decision had been made. No more was heard!

The repairs to the Down line were estimated to take three days. A revised train plan was introduced, taking into account the single line working, and this worked well. After examination the sugar beet pulp train was allowed to go forward leaving behind the derailed vanfit which had suffered considerable damage to its wheels, having run for some distance in a derailed state. It was therefore decided to bring an empty bogie bolster wagon from Whitemoor yard, together with the March crane, and leave the Bobol in the siding at Manea after loading the damaged wagon on it.

Why not take it back with the returning crane, I thought? This seemed like a good idea except that the load would be above the standard loading gauge. No problem. After all this was the fens and there were no overbridges between Manea and March Down yard. There was, however, the Down starting signal at Stonea which was a high signal cantilevered over the Down line.

When the return movement was ready to take place it was accompanied by an inspector who was specially warned to watch out for the Stonea starter and make sure the wagon would clear it. Off it went and some time later the 'Train Out of Section' bell signal was received at Stonea. All seemed to be going well until this was followed by the 2-4 bell signal 'Blocking Back Inside Home Signal'. The wagon had proved too high. What now?

The normal 'out-of-gauge' regulations were primarily focused on the width of large loads to protect adjoining lines. They permitted a load to travel on the wrong line under special bell signals and without a pilotman. Nothing was said about height, so why not use this method to get the load on from Stonea to March? Shown the regulations the driver agreed, the train was sent back through the Stonea crossover and moved on safely to March under the special bell signals. The job was done and nothing further was ever said, just proving that rules and regulations can be interpreted in many ways.

Two Sequels

The Manchester to Harwich boat train used to run via Sheffield, Lincoln, Spalding and March. The middle section, originally the GN&GE Joint line, ran through a predominantly agricultural area and had many signal boxes and level crossings. Of the latter quite a few served no more than farm access tracks and, as such, could be manned by women crossing keepers for a full 24 hours without a break because of the low level of use. Rule 99 provided that the gates must be closed against the road at all times except when road vehicles needed to cross and it was safe for them to do so.

One dark winter evening the boat train, hauled by a Class 37 locomotive, was running up the Joint Line at about 60mph when it ran through a set of large wooden level crossing gates. Fortunately no one was on the crossing, there was no derailment and only minimal damage to the train which stopped and was then allowed to go forward after examination.

When I interviewed the lady crossing keeper about the incident she said she was in the house preparing tea when a car driver rang the gate bell to be let over the line. After checking that no trains were approaching she opened the gates and then, about to close them again, spotted the lights of another car in the distance. As no trains were approaching she decided to let it cross before closing the gates. At that point the kettle started whistling in the kitchen so she went into the house to attend to it and forgot about the gates as she busied herself getting tea. Until the Harwich boat train arrived!

The first sequel arose on the evening of the incident when a chicken farmer who lived near the level crossing and had a large battery henhouse there came out to find that a sizeable wooden strut with metal hinges, torn from one of the level crossing gates, had damaged one of his buildings with devastating effect upon its hen occupants. Our visit next day found the farmer not unreasonable but there was later a claim for the damage, for four dead hens and 4,000 birds off lay for two weeks. The area manager and I at least came away with a gift of fresh eggs!

The lady crossing keeper was given a verbal warning and the matter seemed to be closed until the second sequel cropped up. Several weeks later I was taking the pay out to the signallers and crossing keepers along the Joint Line, accompanied by a lampman who stayed in the van while I was making each delivery. He let slip that the original version of events might not be the truth. The crossing keeper's son had apparently confided in friends on the school bus that on the evening in question he had been working the level crossing gates while his mother was in bed with a railwayman! What happened at the moment of impact we shall never know!

Exhibition Trains

Arranging and running exhibition trains was a complex business as David Crathorn and Geoff Body recall.

The Chair

Exhibition trains were run very successfully by Barry Gray. Barry carefully planned the itinerary to suit clients' specifications, researched the stations where the exhibition train would call, noting how the train should be berthed, the type and length of electrical leads wanted and the water connections required. He also identified the various exhibitors' requirements for parking, signs, off-train reception arrangements and the receipt and storage arrangements for equipment and documentation. The task of timing these trains, finding traction, stock and crews was equally complex.

With so many details to be communicated to rail staff at the various stations used, it is no surprise that Barry and his assistant produced very comprehensive instructions, running to many pages, which were despatched by the railway letter service to all concerned. As a result of this detailed activity those who chartered the BR exhibition train were very pleased with the results and some made repeated bookings.

A particular feature of these operations was the appointment of a train manager. He would virtually live on each train, so as to ensure it was worked as booked and to cope immediately with any problems that arose. Several men, including former area managers, fulfilled the train manager role with distinction.

One especially memorable experience was after Mirror Group News had hired the exhibition train in order to promote sales in the South West of England. The departure time from Paddington had to be carefully planned so as not to interfere with booked trains. As that departure time neared, there was no sign of Robert Maxwell, the then chairman of MGN, who was to travel with the train. Finally he arrived and there was a scramble to get him aboard and the train away.

As the train ran west, Robert Maxwell called for 'His Chair', in order to have his sales meeting at the front of the train en route. Unfortunately this special chair had been hastily stowed in the rear brake at the last minute. There was nothing for it but to carry the bulky chair the full length of the train, with the equally bulky Maxwell closely supervising, when not actually carrying it himself. History does not record if the MGN sales meeting was a success, but the exhibition train certainly ran well.

The Package

An exhibition train of a rather different sort was one of the principal features of the celebrations in 1985 of the Great Western Railway's 150th anniversary, GWR150 as it was known. WR public relations manager Ron Drummond gave Geoff Body the task of exploiting the opportunity for sales of souvenirs and other items during the several weeks of the event. This sounded simple enough but the first shock was being left to design from scratch a sales coach that would supplement the display vehicles on the train, and then persuading the C&W staff at Canton to fit it out. This accomplished, suitable sales items had to be selected, suppliers consulted, display cases filled, accounting arrangements made and staff recruited and trained. A notable feature of my design, judge it as you will, was that train visitors could not reach the exit without passing the sales counter!

With supplies organised, a logical development was to arrange selling at the lecture programme that was another feature of the GWR150 event, to set up a mail order facility and to supply sales items via travel centres. We even produced our own sets of postcards featuring period railway posters when we found that a colleague had a collection of the latter in his attic.

The opening event at Paddington was a great success with a large number of visitors and excellent sales, the latter meaning a hurried early morning restocking from Bristol the following day. From then on I chased the train in my van to locations as far apart as Snow Hill and Penzance, doing countless support tasks including such difficult ones as being unable to get up to our

Interior of the sales coach on the GWR150 exhibition train.

coach at Barry Island and having to restock it over a fence and through a small sliding upper window.

The sales activity made a fine profit and contributed to the considerable goodwill engendered by the whole event. The arrangements worked incredibly well and I recall only one slight hiccough. This was at York, one of the locations added to the original itinerary. Like the others it was to be opened by the Mayor who was just about to board the train when I got a nasty shock. Now this was the period of frequent bomb scares and there, hidden in a corner, was what was clearly a 'suspect package'. With alacrity and authority I halted the official party only to turn round and face a sheepish steward who admitted that the bag contained his sandwiches!

Far West

Until it became part of his commercial responsibility, Cornwall had just been a holiday destination for Geoff Body. He soon found out how valuable its traffic was.

'Never knew a chap who had so many jobs at once.' This appeared as a postscript on the letter of congratulations which my divisional manager wrote to me when I relinquished acting as his commercial manager at Liverpool Street for pastures new. I had been appointed to a passenger business promotional job at York but then was placed into an even better one as marketing & sales manager for the West of England Division based at

Bristol. My stay there was to prove one of the most interesting and rewarding periods of my career.

Bristol had absorbed the former Plymouth office and divisional manager Henry Sanderson's expanded territory was the huge area from Worcester in the north, Swindon to the east and Weymouth in the south, and then westwards all the way to the Isles of Scilly. It handled the main passenger line services from London via Swindon and via Newbury and the cross-country routes to the holiday areas of Devon and Cornwall, and also a variety of major freight movements ranging from bananas out of Avonmouth Docks to huge volumes of Mendip limestone.

One of my first tasks was to familiarise myself with this vast territory which, apart from holiday visits, was all new ground to me. The two weeks I could devote to this task proved very rewarding. Only one area presented me with problems. This was the triangle lying west of the main line beyond Par and the branch line from there to Newquay. The home of the vast industry of English China Clays, or ECLP, it was a labyrinth of workings and of the freight-only lines and sidings which served them.

Above: St Dennis Junction with the Par–Newquay line on the left and the mineral line link to Meledor Mill and Burngullow heading off to the south.

Right: A double-headed train of sheeted china clay wagons joins the main line at Par.

One source of my difficulties lay in getting any sort of up-to-date map of these lines which were now part of my commercial responsibility. As the extraction process altered, some branches and loading points were closed or moved, and keeping up with the changes was a major task, even for the civil engineer. The other difficulty was the names. The local railwaymen bandied about locations like Parkandillick & Trevalour, Melangoose Mill, West Goonbarrow and Wheal Benallick, which made me feel both slightly bemused and very much the new boy.

This feeling of being a stranger reminded me of an earlier visit to Plymouth in pursuit of Ford car business when I had asked a station porter to mind my case for a few moments. 'Oh, zur,' he said, 'you must be from London. No one down 'ere wun't touch your things.' Plymouth has other memories too like the return journey to Bristol after an official social event involving the whole family. The very likeable chauffeur Ron Hodges drove us and mentioned that assistant divisional manager Clive Rowbury had asked for his dog, Toby, to be brought back at the same time. Now Toby was a huge, amiable boxer who sat in the middle of the front bench seat of the vehicle and eventually, bored with the whole thing, leaned onto me and promptly fell asleep. Nothing would get this massive hound off my shoulder, nor stem the flow of dribble to which boxer's are prone!

Another recollection is of lovable May, the ultra-helpful secretary at Plymouth, telephoning me when fog had grounded my return flight from Scilly after a meeting with the Isles of Scilly Steamship Company who were our agents. 'Mr Rowbury says you are not to worry,' was her message. On my eventual return I thanked him for this piece of thoughtfulness. 'What I actually said,' responded Clive, 'was tell him if he is not back by Monday we will fill his job!'

Of course, understanding of the china clay business duly came, helped by frequent negotiations with the very enterprising senior staff of the clay company. It was so important to BR that one of the two branch lines to the shipment area at Fowey had been closed to allow ECLP to use it for road access in return for a toll payment. Rail still handled large quantities for shipment at Carne Point plus trainloads to the Potteries and other flows. The Parkandillick, Drinnick Mill and Goonbarrow complex alone offered 274,000 tons of rail business annually with the Retew and Carbis branches adding another 173,000 tons to this. The movement pattern was based on trips from loading point to St Blazey for sorting and the provision of main line motive power for the onward journeys from there.

The china clay business was not the only revelation for me in the holiday counties of the West. There, Christmas was hardly over before daffodils were crossing from the Isles of Scilly for despatch from Penzance, while Marazion, notable in my mind as a vantage point for seeing and visiting St Michael's Mount, was the focus of huge loadings of broccoli in the season. Potatoes, too, passed by rail in quantity, the Old Delabole Slate Company despatched some of their output by rail, Watts, Blake, Bearne despatched ball clay, while end of the line Torrington played a sizeable part in the supply of milk to London. To maintain the variety there was even short-haul coal traffic ex-ship at Fremington Quay and moved to the nearby power stations.

The 'Far West', for railwaymen, was not just cliffs, beaches, palm trees and long-disused mining pump houses, but an area of varied and vital freight business.

In the sheltered estuary of the River Fowey wagons of china clay are being unloaded for shipment.

Ten years after passenger trains used these platforms, Torrington is still important for its milk tank forwardings.

Humour

In a busy, varied and often stressful job railwaymen generally managed to see the funny side of life and found that it helped both in their work and in their relationships. Throughout a distinguished career Peter Rayner believed firmly in the importance and benefits of humour, as these incidents he recalls make abundantly clear.

Regulation 25

When I wrote *On and Off the Rails* my old friend Harold Horsfall, former Manchester divisional chief inspector, was alive. Not, as he admitted, alive and well, for he had quite painful arthritis which he very properly ignored as we walked the Dales and in the Lake District. Eventually age caught up and, very close to the end of his life, Harold was in Stockport Royal Infirmary where I visited him along with Bill O'Brien, a senior signalling inspector in Manchester in my day. Bill picked me up at the station and we went to the hospital.

Humour has always mattered to me in terms of management, or just in life. It defuses pain and tension and helps with our emotions, often making the bond between people stronger. In this case both Bill and I were uptight at the sight of the deeply asleep Harold Horsfall and we stopped by his bed in an awkward, affectionate silence. The nurse said, 'You can stay as long as you like gentlemen. It is very unlikely Mr Horsfall will wake to see you.'

We stood for a while longer and eventually Bill, who had been a signalman at Stockport when Harold had been the signalling inspector said, reversing their former roles, 'You weren't very good on Regulation 25. I will be back in a fortnight.' Harold slept on.

I was laughing and near to tears. Humour had helped us through. 'You are right,' I said to the nurse, 'he is deeply asleep.'

That was the last I saw of my old friend and he passed away a few days later.

Mind the Gap

Many station platforms are on a curve so that 'Mind the gap!' is a well-known cry; one of London's originals! When I went to be operating officer of the Southern Region one of the new things I learned was about getting 'Gapped'. Not the same as platform curvature but falling foul of electric current breaks when moving slowly and with bad rail conditions.

I thought mind the gap problems had been left behind me when I went back to Crewe finally in 1986. Gaps were there and I knew, in a road knowledge sense, exactly where they were. Certainly with some traction we had to 'run down' before going through the gap. They were undoubtedly essential to maintaining the electrical supply and to isolating sections for engineering or other maintenance work, but they were a perpetual nuisance to us operators.

Humour I fear again is perhaps disproportionately important to me as I remember the extraordinary mess we made whilst testing braking characteristics at Colwich after the accident there, and during the subsequent investigations. We had put the damaged train back together and did some trial runs at Colwich 38 signal. On one we were unlucky. We put the brake in, or rather at chief inspector Ralph Reynold's instruction the driver put the brake in, and we rolled along, past No.38 signal and onto the North Staffs line towards Stoke, with me commenting over the intercom to Colin Boocock and assorted engineers in the train. Slowly and gently we came to a stand, bang in the middle of the gap. I looked at Peter Olver – Major Peter Olver, the inspecting officer – and saw a twinkle in his eye. 'I'll bet you're glad to be back on the Midland, Peter,' he said. Actually, of course I was!

I got down and stood as my inspectors moved a twelve-coach Blackpool train onto the back of ours and pushed us slowly further onto the branch. As the Blackpool set back a head appeared from a first class window and asked, 'Is this normal?' To which I replied, 'Perfectly normal, sir, part of our emergency drills.' 'Reynold's Gap' the spot became, and always will be to a number of us.

Perhaps the most odd and amusing of the gap stories occurred just outside our house in Stafford. The gap is Crewe side of Stafford No.5. A London-bound train with Euston men had stopped just north of the station and the signalman at No.5 asked a Preston crew on a Down express to see what was wrong with the Up train. They stopped cab to cab and the Preston men said, 'What's up, mate?' To which we are told the Londoner replied, 'Same as you, mate! We are in the ****** gap!

Four's a Crowd

Bill Parker remembers how, in the 1980s, he disregarded the rules in getting a VIP lady back on track.

Receiving the guests for the special train to Wood Green at Kings Cross suburban station for the formal opening of the refurbished Alexandra Palace and the renaming of Wood Green station to Alexandra Palace, area manager Charles Wort and divisional manager Bill Parker awaited the arrival of the guest of honour, the popular actress Liza Goddard.

Divisional manager Bill Parker and Diana Dors – his surprise, but welcome, guest of honour – are the focus of media attention at the renaming of Wood Green station to Alexandra Palace.

As the time arrived for the train's departure, information came through that the VIP's taxi was delayed in Central London traffic. The train had to leave, with Charles Wort hosting the other guests already on board. Imagine his surprise when Bill Parker saw Diana Dors approaching in haste, and telling him that she was on her way to open 'Ally Pally'. Taken aback, he exclaimed, 'But you're not Alvin Stardust's wife!' and was told with a chuckle that she was standing in for Liza.

To redeem his blunder he invited the stand-in VIP to ride in the cab of an outer suburban train about to depart. To make a punctual start and then a special stop at Wood Green, Bill had to override the rules about the usual stop order form, a cab pass for Miss Dors and allowing four people in the cab, one of whom was a well-built traction inspector! He even allowed his guest to 'drive the train' for a few minutes.

In the event everyone enjoyed the ride with Diana jauntily wearing the driver's cap and saying that she had achieved a lifetime's ambition – despite the tight squeeze in the cab!

Solving a Logistical Nightmare

Harry Knox describes an example of the bulk movement at which rail has always excelled, in this case the carriage of 7,000 tons daily of 'blaes' from Bathgate 'bings' to Shieldhall.

Spent shale, otherwise known as 'blaes', was the legacy left in both Mid and West Lothian by the Scottish shale oil industry which operated there from around 1850 until 1963. Vast quantities of oil shale were mined from under a 75-square-mile shale field, in excess of 170 million tons over the life of the industry. This shale, heated in specially designed retorts, gave off a thick 'smoke', actually hydrocarbon gases, which, when cooled and condensed, formed a rich crude oil. The oil, after refining, produced such commodities as naphtha, paraffin, heating and burning oils, lubricating oils, paraffin wax and, a most important commodity, sulphate of ammonia, much in demand as a fertiliser.

The burnt shale, red in colour, and now totally inert, was dumped on waste tips ('bings' in Scotland) alongside each of the oil works. The volume of shale mined equalled the volume of shale being tipped, so the bings were inevitably immense, and in total, twenty-nine such bings were scattered around the Bathgate/Broxburn/West Calder area. Initially considered eyesores and worthless, post-war this spent shale was to assume a considerable value since the weight to volume ratio was good, it was an all-weather material and it compacted well. More importantly, it was cheap and there was plenty of it around!

Bathgate, on the NBR Edinburgh to Glasgow via Airdrie line, lay at the heart of industrial West Lothian, and the yard was, in its heyday, the largest marshalling yard in Scotland, and one of the largest in the UK, being rail-connected to over fifty collieries, a great number of shale mines and pits and nine oil works, plus foundries, iron works, brick works etc. Bathgate shed provided motive power for all traffic requirements arising and had a large number of daily turns for this purpose. As the shale industry folded, and coal working declined, so rail activities at Bathgate likewise contracted. In the mid-1960s the Government, now seriously concerned at the higher-than-average unemployment in this former shale area, instructed British Leyland, the Midlands-based car giant, to construct the new factory to house the expanding Truck & Tractor Division, at Bathgate, and this was duly done. Bathgate yard was rail-connected to the new factory and a new type of rail traffic became the mainstay, with trucks and tractors going out by rail, and trainloads of cars arriving inwards.

In the mid-1960s, under the two-tier management structure in BR's Scottish Region, geographical operating areas were formed and Bathgate became the management centre for one such area. In 1973 I went to Bathgate as terminals & operating assistant (and was later to become area manager) and thus was to be in at the beginning of the big shale contract.

Fast-forward to 1973. The civil engineering company Leonard Fairclough Ltd was awarded the contract to construct the Renfrew Motorway Phase 2, an extension of the M8 motorway, westwards from Glasgow, and this project required a minimum 1.5 million tons of infill. Fairclough's had decided that shale was the right material. A Bathgate-based road haulage contractor, William Griffith (Whitburn) Ltd, had in past times and with an eye to the future, purchased four shale bings, a shrewd move as it turned out, and was by the early 1970s the largest handler of shale blaes anywhere in the UK. Fairclough's needed the equivalent of a bing, and Griffiths just conveniently had one lying spare, their largest, at Deans, a mile or so east of Bathgate.

However, transportation between bing and construction site at Shieldhall in the west of Glasgow posed serious environmental problems, not least of which was the prospect of forty-five heavy tipper lorries making three trips each way daily through the notorious bottlenecks of central Glasgow and the Clyde Tunnel. The latter had proved a serious problem to Griffiths in the past when blaes dust, whipped up from the loaded trucks, clogged up the tunnel air purification system. Even with this intensive use of lorries, the best Griffiths could offer was 2,000 tons per day, delivered to site.

Enter BR and Scottish Region's freight manager D.R. Harries. BR was keen to become involved since Deans bing lay adjacent to the Bathgate/ Airdrie freight line, and with an existing rail connection already in situ. In negotiations with Griffith and Fairclough, BR offered to transport a guaranteed 7,000 tons of shale daily from Deans bing to Shieldhall, five days per week, over a fifteen-month period, and this offer was accepted. Griffith spent some £60,000 constructing a new siding into the heart of Deans shale bing and there provided three loading sidings, each with a rounding connection. Bathgate was to be the hub of this operation.

The management team established locomotive and crew diagrams for this additional traffic. Bathgate had but two Class 20 locomotives allocated, covering five trip diagrams and yard shunting. Additional motive power was needed and this came in the shape of eight Class 25 locomotives working as four units in multiple. Four block trains were made up, each consisting of thirty-six x 21-ton hopper wagons (initially unfitted) and each train carried a payload of 750 tons. Nine trains were to be run over 24 hours every weekday, and this involved careful timetable planning by the HQ train planning section in order to thread these heavy, unfitted trains through the intensive, and time-sensitive, electrified suburban rail services of North Clydeside.

The Bathgate allocation of drivers was increased by three, and five secondmen were recruited. Additional guards were also recruited. This was a very important and high-profile rail working, and from day one all staff at Bathgate pulled out all the stops to ensure things went smoothly. Now, in everyday life at Bathgate, we had enough (and sometimes more than enough) to contend with, since four main lines of railway ran through the Bathgate area, namely the Edinburgh to Glasgow main line (Bo'ness Junction to Saughton Junction), Edinburgh to Airdrie via Bathgate (Bathgate Junction to Caldercruix), the West Coast Main Line Edinburgh to Carstairs (Kingsknowe to Auchengray) and Edinburgh to Glasgow Central (Mid-Calder Junction to Benhar Junction), and so this new shale working posed yet another potential problem. We were not to be disappointed.

The method of working required that an empty train went out on the Up line from Bathgate yard to Deans, and was propelled back into the loading sidings. Here, there would be another train waiting, already loaded, and thus it was just a matter of rounding internally, propelling the loaded train out, and working wrong direction over the Up line, back to Bathgate yard. Griffiths loaded the empty wagons using Chaseside mechanical shovels, and these large machines could, and did, load the thirty-six wagons in under an hour.

The 37-mile journey westward lay over the heavily graded Bathgate to Airdrie freight-only line, not an easy route for a loose-coupled freight train, and at Airdrie the shale trains encountered the North Clyde electric passenger services. At High Street (Bellgrove Junction) the shale took the City Union line to General Terminus and on into Shieldhall yard. There, a discharge facility was constructed for bottom door discharge into a bunker, this unloading taking around an hour. The bunker was capable of holding two or three train loads. The empty trains then returned to Bathgate via the same route.

The problems? Well, a problem was soon to arise with sharp flanges on the 21-ton hopper wagons since the working meant that wear on the wheelsets was uneven because of the line curvature, and the fact that the train was never reversed, so wagons thereafter had to be turned at each preventative maintenance period. Engine failure was, surprisingly, never a serious problem and the class 25s coped very well, but every Saturday each locomotive had to be run light to Haymarket depot for maintenance and inspection. This required the booked single Saturday crew to make four trips to Haymarket, returning by bus each time. This kept them at it for their 8 hours and was never popular. We had to crack down hard on one enterprising crew who, on one particular Saturday, coupled up the eight locomotives and made one run to Haymarket.

Derailments were a recurring feature and, strangely, involved one train running out to Deans at midnight, and always on a Friday night. We had, on several Friday nights, thirty-six wagons off all wheels when propelling into the loading siding. We became adept at re-railing hopper wagons by using the Chaseside loading shovels. These, one on each side and with the wagon balanced, could lift a wagon back onto the rails in seconds. A quick examination by our C&W examiner and the wagons were back into service without delay.

Investigation later revealed that the guards working this turn were rostered for two round trips daily and by the end of the week, sheer carelessness was the cause, but why? Fatigue was not something really understood or recognised at the time, but later, as a rail safety consultant in Australia, I was to be involved in a study to promote the understanding, and effect, of fatigue amongst safety-critical rail shift workers, in conjunction with the University of South Australia and the train crew manager of the National Rail Corporation. Through this most enlightening experience I retrospectively understood the primary cause of the otherwise inexplicable derailments all those years ago at Bathgate.

There was, towards the end of the contract, one main line derailment. The midday train left Bathgate on time, but around 13.00 the signalman at Westcraigs Junction (5 miles to the west) was becoming concerned about its non-appearance. Into the car and away I went until, just after leaving Armadale, at former Woodend Junction, I saw the train at a stand. Abandoning the car, across the fields I ran. The last twenty wagons were standing on the track but immediately ahead...there was no track...merely nineteen wagons on their sides and with shale everywhere. The locomotives were missing but it transpired that, after observing the absolute destruction, the crew had uncoupled and run forward to Westcraigs to raise the alarm. The guard had secured the brake in his van and had gone back to protect his train.

What had happened is this: the hopper coupled to the rear locomotive had broken away and derailed, pulling the next wagon into derailment as well. This second wagon had turned to lie across the track on its side and then, being propelled by the momentum of the remaining wagons, had acted like a bulldozer and cleared rails, sleepers and everything out of its path. Rails, twisted out of shape, were wrapped around telegraph poles and lay in adjoining fields, shattered sleepers littered the site, and the roadbed was as smooth as if it had been purposely levelled. A broken coupling was discovered, still attached to the leading hopper, but nothing to point to why derailment then occurred could be found. It was a 'scorched earth' incident with any and all clues destroyed.

Damage to the Up line was minimal, however, and we thereafter maintained the service by dint of single line working until the Down line was completely relaid. This relaying was not helped when the new rail which had been run out during the week, ready for weekend installation, was found to have completely disappeared. All that remained, at regular intervals, were small heaps of molten steel where the rail had been cut into manageable lengths and removed. A nearby encampment of 'travellers' had also, strangely, disappeared!

The shale contract was a resounding success. The shale was delivered in sufficient quantity each day to maintain the scheduled motorway extension plan. Fairclough were extremely satisfied with the rail operation. Griffiths, with this single £250,000 contract, enjoyed a handsome return and were highly delighted, particularly at being spared the logistical headache of an intensive road haulage operation. The rail operation was undoubtedly a real bonus for a transportation challenge which could have proved an environmental nightmare. A little over 2 million tons of shale was transported halfway across Scotland in this fifteen-month operation, with little or no environmental impact, and we rail operators at Bathgate emerged with pride, and with not a little additional experience under our belts.

The Tramway

In the 1960s the former London, Tilbury & Southend Railway lines along the north bank of the Thames produced an exceptional level of freight and passenger traffic as Geoff Body was to find out very soon after arrival at the LT&S Line headquarters.

After fourteen years working on the railway, three of them undergoing the special training given to traffic apprentices, I thought I was well qualified to take on almost any job in the various commercial and operating activities of the industry. However, nothing had quite prepared me for my new appointment as head of the Sales & Development section on 'The Tramway'. The Tramway was the name given by its detractors and those envious of its earning power to the modest 39-mile main line from London's Fenchurch Street terminus to Shoeburyness and its loop line via Tilbury. Under BR Eastern Region control this small but busy area had been selected as a pilot scheme for a new 'line' organisation. J.W. Dedman was appointed as the first Line Traffic Manager (LT&S).

The first hour after I arrived at the line headquarters in Saracen's Head House, off Fenchurch Street, was normal enough, just touring the offices, meeting the staff and so on. Then came the bombshell from my predecessor Geoff Foulger, now promoted to sales assistant and greeting me with the words, 'Welcome. The budget submission is due in and the papers are on your desk.' I knew little about the line's existing traffics and even less about its potential but everyone was too busy to rescue me and I managed as best I could. Lesson learned, for this was the LT&S management style viz, 'Get on with it and you'd better be right'.

Both of the LT&S routes carried a great deal of commuter traffic. All the stations, from those in the Borough of Southend westwards, filled the morning Up trains, some travellers transferring to the branch lines from Upminster or to the parallel Metropolitan and District lines, others changing at Barking for the Tottenham & Hampstead line. In their thousands these commuters made no secret of their expectations and demanded constant attention from the operating superintendent Bob Arnott downwards.

At the LT&S centenary celebrations back in 1956 the Railway Executive chairman Sir Reginald Wilson had been jokingly offered the mayoral chain of Southend if he could complete the promised electrification of the line within two years, but the first electric train was not seen until 6 November 1961 and the long-awaited new electric timetable did not come into operation until 18 June 1962. In the meantime Plaistow Motive Power Depot had a great struggle to keep the worn-out stable of steam locomotives operating while the new East Ham emu depot was built, brought into service and then coped with the inevitable teething problems. The station staff dealt with the changes amazingly well; at headquarters operators Jim Urquhart, Les Lovett and Frank Southgate made sure that failing emus were attended to without putting vital freight services in jeopardy, and our public relations officer, Percy Gillett, had to be at his smoothest and most persuasive in explaining our initial failings.

At that time the love affair between Londoners and the whelks and cockles of Leigh-on-Sea or the delights of Southend's pier and Kursaal was very strong and filled many evening and weekend trains with Cockney folk intent on a good time. Southend Central's traditional departure warning handbell proved surprising effective in getting tipsy revellers on board the last homeward-bound train of the day. Other extra business came from our passenger representatives who brought in a lot of party traffic for the excellent Fred Rolfe to arrange in my office and we had frequent boat trains from St Pancras to Tilbury which were in the experienced hands of my deputy Charlie Dicks.

From the raised level platforms at Fenchurch Street the main line headed east above old spice warehouses and the evocatively named French Ordinary Court. There was a wagon hoist link to the old Royal Mint Street depot followed by siding connections to the huge warehouses at Haydon Square and Commercial Road. On one occasion in the months before Christmas the latter was near-filled with stored Christmas puddings, surely a scenario the Goons would have exploited had they known.

It was on the LT&S that I got my first taste of the complications of dealing with docks traffic. When the East and West India Docks were forced by competition to build their new dock at Tilbury, an agreement was reached with the LT&S under which no road access would be provided. Instead all traffic would be conveyed by rail at a special rate to Commercial Road where the railway would build a new warehouse for it on the site of an old German church graveyard. The warehouse was built in 1886 with ten trains booked to serve it each day and the dock company guaranteeing a minimum of 200,000 tons a year to justifying the building costs. In later years the level of traffic declined and lengthy negotiations were held with the Port of London Authority, who now owned Tilbury and were anxious to reduce or avoid the penalty that had to be paid on tonnage shortfalls.

Traffic was exchanged between rail and water at the British Waterways Board's Regents Canal Dock which adjoined Stepney East station. From there we had inherited the original cable-worked route of the London & Blackwall Railway which ran via Millwall Junction to our portion of the docks and sufferance wharf at Poplar.

Beyond Barking the main line headed for Upminster while the Tilbury Loop followed the river via the new Ripple Lane marshalling yard. The section between Dagenham Dock and Low Street produced massive quantities of freight traffic and was home to a host of companies bearing

Back in 1890, the 9.10 from Southend to Fenchurch Street and the 17.50 return were the crack trains on the LT&S line. Even electrification in 1962 could only better their times by a few minutes.

LONDON TILBURY AND SOUTHEND RAILWAY.

SOUTHEND-ON-SEA

AND

LONDON

(FENCHURCH STREET)

IN

FIFTY MINUTES,

BY THE

UPMINSTER LINE EXPRESS,

WEEK   {9.10 a.m from SOUTHEND.
DAYS.   {5 5 p.m from FENCHURCH STREET.

FAST TRAINS FOR BUSINESS MEN.

WEEK DAYS.

	A.M.	A.M.		Sats. only P.M.	P.M.	P.M.
SOUTHEND............dep.	7 48	9 10	FENCHURCH ST. dep.	2 8	5 5	6 8
FENCHURCH ST. ...arr.	8 50	10 0	SOUTHEND ....arr.	3 12	5 55	7 15

PERIODICAL TICKETS.

	ONE WEEK.	TWO WEEKS.	ONE MONTH.	TWO MONTHS.	THREE MONTHS.
	£ s. d.	£ s. d.	£ s. d.	£ s. d.	£ s. d.
SECOND CLASS	0 16 0	1 9 0	2 3 0	3 15 0	4 6 0
FIRST CLASS	1 5 0	2 2 0	3 3 0	5 10 0	6 6 0

well-respected industrial names who had private sidings or siding access along what was little over 13 miles of railway. Between Dagenham Dock and the river lay the huge estate of S. Williams & Co. which had its own rail network and shunting locomotives. One of the nice memories of our links with this company is of being invited to join in the Thames welcome of Sir Francis Chichester from the deck of one of their fleet of tugs.

Dagenham was also important to the LT&S for the huge potential of the Ford Motor Company. At the beginning of the 1960s Fords were receiving their heavy raw materials mostly by ship or by rail and, like Williams, had their own sidings and locomotives. However, the thousands of finished cars bought ex-works by main dealers all over the country were moved almost entirely by road using delivery drivers and three large operators of car transporter vehicles. Our commercial manager, Ted Taylor, was determined to have some of this business.

It took over a year to visit dealers and persuade them to transfer their business to rail and then to get Fords to take responsibility for delivery themselves and pocket the advantages of service and cost we proved we could give them. Before another year was out this campaign had been expanded to embrace a prestige daily parts train from Dagenham to Halewood, which was treated as part of the Ford production line and required to achieve the punctuality which that status necessitated.

The section of line on to Grays produced vast quantities of traffic, particularly timber, petroleum products and various types of cement. From Frog Island came the packaged timber of the Rainham Timber Co. and Purfleet had sidings to several busy wharf installations, Esso and Shell depots, Thames Board Mills and Van den Burgh & Jurgens. Grays itself was the home of Thomas Hedley & Co. and Thos. Ward's shipbreaking activity. If only I had taken up the offer of a redundant ship's lifeboat at a price of £1 per foot length or bought some of the lovely brass ship fittings which had seen so much of the world!

Tunnel, Lafarge and the Cement Marketing Company all produced cement at works on the approach to Grays. As the new Presflo wagons became available we carried more and more of this business and I shall not forget the opportunity to peer into one of the CMC cement kilns where the temperature reached a truly frightening level of around 1,000 degrees! Another memory is of a visit to my old friend and colleague Jim Burnham who was the goods agent for this whole complex. His wife Rene showed me what happened to her washing in an area dominated by cement works, but

despite this Jim always looked immaculate. While I had a bad habit of defusing difficult situations by stretching out the process of lighting my pipe, Jim would reply to unwanted questions by saying, 'It's no use asking me, I'm just a simple East Anglian!'

Beyond Grays boat trains used the connection at Tilbury

This Esso asphalt plant at Purfleet was just one of the many waterside activities along the north bank of the Thames which was served by the LT&S line.

North Junction to get to the liner berths. Normal passenger trains continued into the Tilbury Riverside terminus from which a frequent ferry service crossed the Thames to Gravesend. The trains continuing to Southend reversed direction at Tilbury Riverside and went forward towards Stanford-le-Hope which controlled access to the Thames Haven freight branch.

The single line to Thames Haven yard had originally opened in 1855 with passenger trains connecting with steamer services on to Margate. The opening of Tilbury docks killed the line's port ambitions but the area became home to the Kynoch munitions production and, after 100 years of life, to the Mobil oil refinery, two large Shell depots and Fisons fertiliser works. Full train loads of 100-ton bogie tank wagons ran regularly to places like Rugby and Rowley Regis, interspersed with bulk fertiliser movements to Immingham and Avonmouth.

The eastern end of the LT&S line terminated at Shoeburyness where there was a rail link to the Ministry of Defence depot. Through Southend Borough our frequent electric train service and a simple single fare of threepence per station enabled us to compete with the local bus operation to the latter's considerable annoyance. Apart from army traffic there was not so much freight business at this end of the line but we did have an important and profitable Agreed Flat Rate with E.K.Cole & Co. for the parcels movement of their output of plastic toilet seats!

Despite its comparatively tiny size, the LT&S was a highly active and profitable railway activity which worked me very hard, taught me an incredible amount and treated me more than fairly. My family life had inevitably been affected by a constant, irregular and demanding work pattern but the reward came when staff officer Stan Eccles summoned me to his office, put on such a threatening mien that I began to fear the worst, and then offered me a promotion that jumped a grade.

The Season

Railways carried a great deal of seasonal traffic – fish, meat, game, sugar beet, grain and so on. Here Ray Unwin recalls the seasonal summer arrangements for Cambridgeshire fruit.

My forty-year journey from a sort of bag carrier to the LNER's medical officer to senior operating officer included several milestones and, I would like to think, a few achievements. At one period I was involved with the Cambridgeshire fruit traffic season, the connection starting back in the thirties when I was a child waiting for my tea because Father, in common with numerous other railwaymen of all grades, was working overtime on fruit loading at Swavesey or Long Stanton stations on the Cambridge to St Ives branch.

From that point my memory moves 'fast forward' to 1948 and my job in the Cambridge district freight train office. There the short soft fruit season provided me with welcome relief from the most boring job ever, that of sorting and checking around 200 guards' journals for the mandatory 'Freight Train Group Return'. My sole consolation came from the knowledge that my predecessor came to the job after piloting a jet fighter, and he coped!

The main soft fruit season was only some six to eight weeks long but during that time large quantities of strawberries ripened ready for the markets. These were consigned in individual 2lb chip baskets fitted with a handle, not the easiest of items to carry and stack without bruising the fruit. The baskets had to be loaded individually into vanfits, from four or five rows high at the wagon ends to a single row at the doors. These were then moved to destination on a mix of special and booked services via the vast Whitemoor marshalling yard at March. Loadings varied from day to day owing to crop and weather conditions but my morning report to operating headquarters, then based at Shenfield, might cover as many as sixty wagons on a good night.

The Cambridge division prepared for the season by selecting extra guards and temporary inspectors, using the latter because the placement of wagons for loading in station yards was important to the marshalling process. Strawberries are a perishable crop and, predictably, the growers all wanted to go on picking as late as possible and still get their fruit to the markets early so as to command the best prices. This meant hectic afternoons at the forwarding stations, but disciplined loading times were the key to achieving punctual next morning arrivals. The ringing of a big brass bell meant 'close the doors and let's go'.

The normal pattern of services included two trains off the St Ives loop – Oakington, Long Stanton, Swavesey, St Ives and Somersham – and two more off the Wisbech branch – Smeeth Road, Emneth, Wisbech East and the Upwell Tramway. The latter ran along the roadside and former Wisbech Canal out to Upwell and its route through the fields and orchards meant especially heavy loadings from its depots. Until 1929 this unique line had also had a passenger service and even afterwards had a service of up to six trains each way worked by Y6 0-4-0 and then J70 0-6-0 'tram' engines until 1952 when Drewry 204hp diesels took over. A 'Fruit Traffic Office Van' was used to drop a clerk at each depot in the morning so that invoicing could take place right up to the moment the loaded vans got back to Wisbech.

When the new mechanised marshalling yard was built at Whitemoor in 1929–33 the old Norwood yard was retained for handling special traffics requiring more careful shunting than could be given by the two main hump yards. Such traffic was passed over a 'knuckle' into one of the fourteen sorting sidings by a small team consisting of a head shunter and two other shunters, the one in the points frame responding to the head shunter's destination signals. The yard was always busy in the late afternoons with fragile, urgent and other special loads to be shunted for transfer to the pattern of evening despatches. It was here that the fruit traffic was handled, shunted carefully over the knuckle but with not a moment wasted in order to ensure despatch on the booked Class C express services from around 7.00 to 9.00p.m.

Cambridgeshire generally supplied the northern markets where the prices were best and the fruit went forward on the booked and special express freight services to Manchester Ducie Street, Newcastle New Bridge Street, and to Leeds and the West Riding. There was also a special fruit season train to Leicester leaving Histon at 4.27p.m. and running via Huntingdon and Kettering but this never loaded very well and was the first of the special workings to be withdrawn each season. Everyone was geared to give priority to such perishable commodities and customer complaints were very few.

I never recall the fruit season without a very special traffic coming to mind. Each year Baxter's Fruit Products of Fochabers, way up in the north of Scotland, bought the crop of a massive field of strawberries near Wisbech. This provided a daily loading which received a priority bordering upon that usually reserved for the royal saloon! A good-condition CCT (covered carriage truck) was used and this was 'tripped' to March for attaching to the rear of the 5.15p.m. overnight Colchester–Edinburgh express which ran via the East Coast Main Line. The movement was monitored throughout, its profitability never really considered.

Eventually the Fochabers traffic went to provide return lorry loads for the Aberdeen meat, another former rail business. Road transport also eroded the rail carryings of strawberries, primarily by being able to offer later loading times, and the Cambridgeshire crop, like that from Cheddar and other places, quietly disappeared into the sunset so far as railways were concerned.

Off to the Tower with Them

Colin Driver recalls an incident at the opening of the refurbished Peterborough station.

At the formal opening in the 1980s of the newly refurbished Peterborough station by Sir Peter Parker, several of the guests were members of the regional Disabled Travellers Panel. The panel had been set up a year or so earlier by

Watched by area manager Charles Milner, chairman Sir Peter Parker emerges from his inspection of the disabled toilet at the rebuilt Peterborough station, smiling at the advice he had had from equally amused, but unrelated, Barbara Parker.

general manager Frank Paterson with myself as chairman and charged with taking into account the special needs of handicapped people in making rail journeys.

Led by area manager Charles Milner, Sir Peter's party inspecting the new station included the lady lay panel member who was very experienced in the needs of handicapped people. On going into the new disabled toilet, Sir Peter was somewhat taken aback when she told him that the facilities were inadequate and, smiling, asked him how he would like his wife to have to use an unforgiving concrete floor to remove underclothes, as she would for her handicapped daughter.

Momentarily speechless, Sir Peter asked for a solution and was told a low bench would work well. He also received the suggestion that the regional architects should go to the Tower – at Blackpool – which in her experience had some of the best disabled toilets in the country. The chairman, in his inimitable manner, responded, 'What a splendid idea,' but added the rider that it should be the Tower of London instead!

A Taste of the Wild West

In August 1963, from the remote Leatherslade Farm near Oakley, Bucks, a gang of fifteen masked robbers succeeded in stealing £2.6 million in used banknotes from the Glasgow to London Euston travelling Post Office mail train at a point near Ledburn. The train driver, Jack Mills, was seriously injured and died seven years later. The district's senior operating officer 'on call' at the time, Bill Parker, describes the events of that fateful night.

The bedside telephone rang in the middle of the night, not unusual in our household during the modernisation of the West Coast Main Line in the 1960s. The voice of the deputy chief controller at the London Euston Divisional Control Office said very calmly, 'Boss, the Up Mail has been stopped between Leighton Buzzard and Cheddington and robbed.' Knowing that my staff knew I was an avid enthusiast of western films, my initial response was to reply (but in stronger language), 'You must be joking. Buckinghamshire is not Texas; there are no cowboys or Jesse James!'

Having quietly assured me it really was not a joke, my caller explained that the Up mail train had been irregularly stopped by a red signal at Seers Crossing between Leighton Buzzard and Chedddington, the front of the train had been moved forward about half a mile to the Bridego railway bridge; that a gang of robbers had raided the postal vehicles and stolen millions of pounds; that they had beaten up the driver who was badly injured and was being taken to hospital; that the local district inspector and on-call station master were on their way to the site; that all four lines had been blocked to enable the police to start investigations; that the engineering departments had been advised; and that alternative arrangements were being planned for the passenger, parcels and freight train service. At that stage it was not known how the signal had gone to red.

As soon as I had taken in this dramatic information I asked my assistant to go to the control office and take charge there while I went directly to the site. The journey there in a civil police car, with siren and blue light in full force, was accomplished in just over 30 minutes. It gave me a brief respite to collect my thoughts and prepare to deal with a situation totally different to anything I had encountered before.

Shortly after my arrival the assistant chief constable (operations) of the BT police arrived and joined his and Bucks county police force members. They were followed very shortly afterwards by Post Office investigators and later by a chief superintendent from Scotland Yard. The latter arranged for his forensic team to start to examine the site including the ballast and surrounding area, and with the locomotive and coaches remaining in situ.

The train crew, except for the severely injured driver, and the signalmen and district inspector were given, in my presence, an initial verbal interrogation by the BT police and local offices, and the position of the signalling equipment was noted.

The district signal & telecommunications engineer conducted a thorough examination of the signalling equipment and found out how it had been cleverly tampered with. The police and myself were present and were given an explanation of what had been done.

After less than a couple of hours, the police chiefs of both forces agreed to permit the locomotive and coaches to be moved by another locomotive from the Up Fast line into Cheddington station sidings, where for about a week the forensic experts and Post Office investigators continued to attempt to find evidence. Once the train had been cleared from the Up Fast line, the Up Slow and Down Fast and Down Slow lines were reopened with a temporary speed restriction operating throughout the site area. The police experts continued to look for evidence on the track and in the area of the hold-up, being protected from the passing trains by railway platelayers. With my local district inspector in charge there all went effectively and safely.

By this time the police had a complete understanding of the signalling and the interference carried out by the robbers. Their attention was then concentrated on the locomotive and coaches in Cheddington sidings and this enabled the train service to be operated at line speed on all four lines through the site.

Nonetheless, as an operator, although recognising the importance of the forensic work, my objective at the time was to get the locomotive and coaches back into service as quickly as possible. After a couple of days, I started to try to put pressure on the Met's chief superintendent to at least release the locomotive. I felt rather like a child who had lost his football over the garden fence and was asking, 'Can I have my engine back?' The chief superintendent, a great guy who clearly was getting tired, gave me a sterner and a slightly more irritable response at our daily conference as each day passed. Neither of us took offence over this matter. We recognised we both had an important job to do and I conceded that, in the circumstances, his need was greater than mine! In any event it would hardly have been appropriate to risk being accused of impeding police enquiries!

The robbery was an audacious and quite villainous piece of work but one modest positive feature was the really superb cooperation between the railwaymen and police forces involved.

A Tale of Railway Staff Cars

Railway cartage vehicles were well maintained and fit for purpose but the same could not always be said for staff cars, as David Ward explains.

Before two-car families became commonplace in the 1980s, BR provided staff cars for its salesmen, officers and others who needed to make journeys as part of their job and which could not conveniently be made by train. After the 1980s it became usual for car journeys to be made in the staff's own cars with the owners' costs covered by a mileage payment.

BR's policy towards staff cars was extremely frugal. Every driver had to pass a road test conducted by the BR road motor engineer's MOT inspector who was qualified to pass out lorry and van drivers for BR goods and parcels services

To be carried in, but not attached to, the Statutory Driving Licence	BRITISH RAILWAYS E REGION	B.R. 14114

MOTOR DRIVER'S DOMESTIC LICENCE

Name (in full) **BODY, GEOFFREY**

Station **LTMO LT&G**   Dept. **FENCHURCH STREET**

Groups of Vehicles authorised to drive	Examiner's Signature	Date
Group 1. Rigid vehicles up to and including 3 tons capacity		
Group 2. Articulated vehicles up to and including 3 tons capacity		
Group 3 Rigid vehicles exceeding 3 tons capacity ..		
Group 4. Articulated vehicles exceeding 3 tons capacity		
Group 5. Tractors including articulated tractive units when used for hauling drawbar trailers		
Group 6. Road Motor Horse Boxes		
Group 7. *Private Car*	*A.E. Nick*	13·3·61

The holder of this licence is not authorised to drive any type of British Transport Commission vehicle other than stated above and is not authorised to drive on the Highway unless he holds a Statutory driving licence.

for a civilian licence but was not permitted to pass out car drivers. A BR staff member therefore had to have two licences to be permitted to drive a railway car. This procedure was apparently necessary to obtain the most favourable insurance terms, which were third party only. In addition only basic car models were purchased which were maintained by the road motor engineer at the district workshops. These cars were kept for up to fifteen years with engine and body overhauls carried out until the car was totally worn out.

The consequence of this policy was that basic Ford Prefects and Anglias were in service long after they had ceased to be produced. These basic models had no heaters, no screen washers, and windscreen wipers worked by air which operated at an uneven speed. In winter not only did the driver and his passengers freeze but it was necessary every few miles to stop and clean the windscreen.

These old cars were the butt of much humour and the cause of some interesting incidents. A senior salesman in the Leeds district had reason to visit a large scrap merchant at Bradford Adolphus Street depot to discuss a demurrage account. He parked his Ford Prefect outside the scrap merchant's office but when he came out of the office after concluding his business he found his car gone from where he had left it. Looking around he saw the yard foreman heading his way who, when within speaking distance, said, 'Sorry mate, I can only give you £10 for your car for the value of the tyres.' From the age and state of the car the foreman had assumed it had been delivered for scrapping and had picked the car up with a grab and deposited on the top of a pile of other scrapped cars.

In another incident the divisional commercial manager at Norwich was provided with a chauffeur-driven Ford Anglia. One day he had to visit a grain merchant at Kennett for an appointment with the chairman of a major brewery. When business was concluded the chairman asked if he could be given a lift to Newmarket. 'Yes,' was the immediate reply, but it was then found that the chairman's portly size could not be fitted into the Ford Anglia and amid much embarrassment a taxi had to be sent for.

These old cars were not safe if they could be coaxed above 50mph because their drum brakes were weak. They were also difficult to drive, being without synchromesh on the gears and not having power steering. In winter it was the driver's responsibility to drain the radiator at night and then refill it in the morning because this was cheaper than antifreeze. Not surprisingly the move towards using personally owned cars with a mileage payment was widely welcomed.

Summer Fever

Serving as it did the long coastline of the south of England 'the Southern' carried incredible numbers of holidaymakers. Fernley Maker recalls what summer weekends were like when he worked at Bude soon after nationalisation.

When I joined the Southern Railway in 1939 station masters were quite lordly creatures and when ours at Plymouth Friary made one of his occasional and very formal visits to the goods office I was reproved by the chief clerk for failing to stand up. Mind you H.C. Ford was a large and portly fellow, much concerned with his dignity and affecting a white top, naval fashion, on his uniform cap in summer.

My next station master, at Okehampton, was equally memorable, but this time for a mournful countenance and an exceedingly dour outlook on life in general. He wore brown boots with his official navy-coloured uniform and observed of the current cricket test series, 'We shall not win. We do not eat enough meat!' My other memory of Okehampton is that the Meldon Quarry signalman 'Bunker' Harris was the local bookie's runner and helped me win 25s on *My Love* in the Derby.

For a period just after nationalisation I was at Bude, a very busy station at that time although evidence of its existence has now entirely disappeared. Just under 230 miles from Waterloo, the small Cornish seaside town was a popular holiday resort and its station was busy during the week with all the traditional railway traffics, and then quite hectic at weekends during the summer. Not only were there large numbers of holidaymakers to deal with but also the Z Reservists who arrived for training courses at a former wartime camp at Cleave, near Morwenstow.

The prelude to the weekend was the departure on Friday nights of the special train carrying the reservists who had completed their fortnight's training. The next batch would then arrive late on Saturday or sometimes on Sunday. When troop trains were running the signal box would be kept open all night but siding accommodation at the station was limited and the track circuits and points locking made it difficult to use it 'creatively'. With space being required for freight wagons, including materials for the new gas works, the empty stock for the London trains and the vans from the pigeon specials which periodically arrived from the Midlands, a second locomotive sometimes had to be steamed on Sunday mornings to tidy everything up ready for Monday and the start of a new week.

In addition to the station master, Bude had two booking clerks, a goods clerk, two signalmen, two guards, two porters, a shunter, a checker and three motor drivers. In the booking office we had to arrive for the early turn at 6.15a.m. on summer Saturdays in time to collect tickets from the inwards train which had left Waterloo some 6 hours before. Some of its passengers needed to leave their suitcases as 'Left Luggage' until they could access their accommodation and no sooner were these booked in and stored than the early turn man, still yawning, would have two or three barrow loads of parcels to 'sheet up' (i.e. list) ready for the delivery vans to load up at 8.30a.m. Next, a collection of goods invoices had to be sorted ready for the goods clerk to collect.

The first train out was the 7.58a.m. which had good connections for Waterloo and for the North via Bristol, and was usually well patronised. As well as booking the tickets, the clerk on duty would also have to deal with telephone enquiries and callers for parcels or left luggage. He also had to make sure that the takings from the previous day were put in the travelling cash safe on this train or face the wrath of the cashier at Exeter. The spring door between the booking and parcels offices must have banged a hundred times on a typical Saturday morning!

There was no let up in the pace before it was time to prepare for the first of the three morning through trains from Bude to Waterloo at nine o'clock. Each of these services had reservable seats but quite often the formation of the train had been changed and its coaches did not match the seat charts, with much last-minute confusion resulting. The 11.17a.m. arrival meant collecting more tickets and excess fares and facing up to another load of parcels. With the daily ticket and cash balance to be done as well – a good hour's work even if the figures balanced first time – these parcels were more often than not locked in the waiting room which was pressed into use for the seasonal surge in parcels traffic, and left there until the pressures eased a bit.

The end of the early turn was now getting near and not before time as the office had no facilities for making tea or handwashing and what refreshment the harassed clerk enjoyed was a matter of haste and his own ingenuity. However, before the late turn man came on at 1.00p.m. the 6-ton goods lorry would arrive with a full load of 'Luggage in Advance' items which had been collected from various hotels. The driver's collection sheets had been prepared the previous day along with the luggage labels but the latter had now to be linked with the individual bags and suitcases with the fervent hope that there would be none of either left over.

The late turn on summer Saturdays was equally busy, the highlight being the arrival of the Atlantic Coast Express, the Southern's famous multi-portion holidaymakers' service. The early turn man would then be back for a long, messy day on the Sunday when he would work 9.00a.m. to 1.00p.m., 2.00p.m. to 4.00p.m., 5.00p.m. to 6.45p.m. and 10.00p.m. to 10.45p.m. There were three trains in and out and if it was wet these would be exceptionally well patronised by holidaymakers intent on keeping out of the rain. There was also the large platform clock to wind after the 2.35p.m. departure and a bit of tidying up from the earlier pressures, but once the last local service was back at 10.15p.m. it was finally time to turn out the lights, lock up and go home.

Geoff Body's first supernumary appointment after traffic apprentice training was at Clacton-on-Sea as assistant station master to Dick Dennis.

From Monday to Friday Clacton was just an ordinary terminal station with four platforms to deal with its commuter business into London and a sprinkling of day visitors. It served the town itself and the sedate area of Holland-on-Sea just to the north and the uninhibited Jaywick Sands to the south, where the Butlins camp was situated. The only non-routine business during the week was in preparation for the weekend when the station would be transformed by the sheer number of carefree holidaymakers arriving and departing.

The advance work involved scheduling every arriving service along with details of the next working of the locomotive, its crew, the rolling stock and the guard, and then typing this up so that the platform staff could all have a copy. Thursday and Friday then produced the first increase in pace when our local sales representative went to the office provided for us at Butlins to sell advance tickets, and the early loads of PLA – Passengers' Luggage in Advance – started to appear.

From about 7.00a.m. each summer Saturday the incoming trains would begin to arrive, initially the booked service from Liverpool Street and then the first of the specials, usually from the Northamptonshire or Bedfordshire direction via Cambridge and Marks Tey. On a day that boded well we could quickly have the passengers shepherded through the ticket barriers, the loco released, the stock stabled or ready for its return working and the crew checked to make sure they knew theirs. On a bad day the guard might be a stand-in for someone who had reported sick and prove unable to take his scheduled outward service because he 'didn't know the road'. No alternative but to 'rob Peter to pay Paul', filch a guard from another job, make a few more adjustments and pass the 'repair' task on to the control office. On a really bad day something would come 'off the road' in the carriage sidings, hopefully not at the entrance.

Soon the first Butlin holidaymakers would start queuing for their outward services and by ten o'clock this queue would stretch endlessly along the local streets. The booking office was locked down like a fortress and the clerks just issued the tickets until their thumbs were sore from the dating press and their fingers stained with the masses of coinage. On the platforms Dick Dennis was like the archetypal ship's captain in seemingly calm control while the station staff, inspectors and myself were constantly on the go to foresee, avoid or remedy all the confusion created by the sheer numbers of people, the unending procession of trains and the fallibilities of both.

Children got lost, passengers forgot tickets, luggage had been left on the racks, drivers arrived late but still needed their break, the parcels office was bombarding us with barrow loads of suitcases to be despatched, wheels came off pushchairs; just about everything that could happen did. Somehow we coped and satisfied most of our passengers even if we occasionally had to enlist the aid of the police or ambulance service or just find a shunting pole to hook up the much-loved cuddly toy dropped down between the carriage running board and the platform!

A Weekend with the Monarch

No, not a summons to the palace or to Balmoral, but Mike Phillips' description of life on board one of BR's InterCity land cruises to explore the wonderful scenery of Scotland.

Throughout the 1990s and the first stages of privatisation – Waterman Railways bought out 'Special Trains' in 1995 – there were several land cruise trains, with such grand titles as *The West Highlander*, *Cock o' the North* and everybody's favourite *Monarch of the Glen*. Advertised nationally, passengers could join the trains at Peterborough or York but the clientele were mostly from London and the South East. The land cruises ran to a common timetable path leaving Kings Cross about 19.30 hours on Fridays to tour the main and branch lines in Scotland, returning to London on Sundays in the winter and Mondays in the summer programme.

Trains were formed of seven sleeper coaches, including a pantry vehicle for the attendant, two kitchen vehicles and seven day coaches including some staff accommodation, and a brake area for the train guard. The train speed was limited to 100mph and the schedule took account of the need to provide comfortable running when the sleepers were in use. The number of passengers on each tour was limited to around ninety by a policy of single-berth sleeper occupancy to improve comfort, and of using only window seats in the day coaches to ensure a perfect view of the superb Scottish scenery.

BR staff on board included a hostess, a train/tour manager, a sleeping car attendant, a travelling cleaner and a maintenance supervisor. InterCity On Board Services provided a chief steward, a chef and table/seat service attendants.

A typical journey would begin with the passengers greeted on arrival at Kings Cross and shown to their places by the hostess. When the train departed northbound behind a Class 86 or Class 90 electric locomotive a full dinner would be served with most of the passengers later retiring to their sleeping berths. Some stayed on in the day coaches to view the beautifully floodlit cathedral at Durham.

Re-engined at Newcastle or Edinburgh with two Class 37 diesels, the train departed from the Scottish capital during the early hours of Saturday heading westwards and skirting Glasgow to reach the West Highland line. By breakfast time it was alongside Loch Lomond, soon passing Crianlarich and traversing the Horseshoe Curve near Bridge of Orchy before crossing the desolate Rannoch Moor. Often a true 'Monarch of the Glen', a fine stag, could be seen surveying his kingdom from high on the hillside. Arriving at Fort William the train split with the sleepers detached and shunted into an adjacent platform to be linked with an electrical supply for the overnight stay.

The day coaches then headed for Mallaig, crossing the notable twenty-one-arch viaduct built by McAlpine and offering a fine view down Loch Shiel and of the Glenfinnan Monument. On arrival at Mallaig passengers made their way to the harbour for a trip on the open waters of Loch Nevis, hopefully spotting a seal on the way. Dinner was served on the return journey to Fort William, with the train moving on to Oban the next morning to enable its passengers to enjoy a ferry crossing to the Isle of Mull and a road tour of the island.

A roast beef dinner was served on the next stage from Oban towards Taynuilt, usually at a stop with a view of a herd of Highland cattle, who

Based on the pre-war LNER Northern Belle cruising trains, David Ward's charter train operation ran two main land cruises in Scotland, one serving Kyle of Lochalsh, Skye and Wick, for the Orkneys, and the other Oban, Mull, Iona and then round to Mallaig. The latter was the *West Highlander*, later renamed *Monarch of the Glen*, and seen here powered by No.37401 *Mary Queen of Scots*. Inverness shed had an allocation of thirteen Class 37/4 locomotives of which two were used for these and other specials and for driver training.

There were also two night land cruises running to the Mull of Galloway, the Isles of Scilly (using Penzance as the railhead), and the Cambrian Coast and Tenby. Destinations nearer London were covered by a wide programme of day cruises, on which the three kitchen cars could serve as many as 378 breakfasts, light lunches and dinners, all to silver service standards. The whole activity was very economical in resources and by its efficiency and high standard, brought many onto the railway after not travelling by train for years. (David Ward Collection)

usually proved highly inquisitive. Reversal brought the train back to Oban and on Monday it finally made its way back south, stopping for a brief shopping opportunity in Edinburgh.

These tours worked well and attracted a high number of 'regulars'. Such problems as were encountered were more likely to come from the passengers than from operating difficulties. Here are a couple of examples.

On one Friday a gentleman joined the train along with two charming ladies. It was obvious from the start that the latter had amorous intentions towards their male companion and the train staff began to refer to them as 'The Guildford Three'. The situation remained calm and apparently normal during the scenic part of the tour but back at Edinburgh the train manager found himself faced by the distressed loser in the battle of the sexes. Tearfully she confided that she could stay on the train no longer and he had to make some hurried arrangements to relieve the tension.

Another incident occurred at Oban one Sunday. On the return from the Isle of Mull tour the hostess reported to the train manager that she had 'lost' a male passenger! He had not returned in time for the ferry, the last of the day. Consternation; should the police be informed; what would HQ say when the news reached London next morning? However, with all the other passengers waiting for the evening dinner trip towards Taynuilt, it was decided to take no action until the return back to Oban.

Amazingly when the train got back there was the missing gentleman walking along the platform. He explained that it was his own fault, having been detached from the main party. Asked how he had retrieved the situation he said, 'I was in the Army. I used my initiative and hired a fishing boat to bring me over.' He was a brave man indeed to face a formidable sea trip in darkness and adverse weather conditions but there was general relief that the matter had been so happily resolved.

An operational incident happened at Oban where a shunter was required on Sunday nights to join the sleeper and day portions of the train together. For maximum safety the communicating doors were provided with two locks, one of the key type and the other a bolt, known in railway terms as a 'French Key'. The latter was only accessible from track level before vehicles were brought together.

On this occasion the shunter, who was brought all the way from Glasgow because of a local staff reduction, forgot the French Keys and the train portions were coupled together without direct access between the two. By the time this was discovered the shunter was on his was back to Glasgow and movement between day coach and sleepers could only be made along the platform. Fortunately the train manager was able to enlist the help of the Oban traincrew in splitting the two sections on the Monday morning but they obliged with a smile and the train departed for London right on time.

Road Motor Drivers Save the Day

Railway cartage and terminals staff rarely enjoyed the limelight but often deserved it, as David Crathorn's account shows.

In 1970 the massive Lawley Street goods depot had been partitioned. The BR Sundries Division had been given the top half fronting Lawley Street, including the cavernous sundries shed, new and old offices, a new canteen, road motor premises and a police office. The BR Full Load goods depot (later Freightliners Ltd) occupied the far end with an entrance to Landor Street, which ran along one side. This depot was mainly in the open but it had the Metal Shed, which became the Inland Port, and two sets of brick offices, one for the supervisors and another for the checkers who held a large stock of pre-printed wagon labels.

The movement of all wagons was arranged by attaching a label to both sides of the wagon showing the destination station or siding, and beneath that the routeing and one or more marshalling yards that the wagon should pass through. Most freight trains followed the traditional routes developed many years before, and connections in yards had also been built up to minimise wagon transit times. An example of this was a wagon carrying Cyril Lord carpets in a BD container from Donagadee to Manchester Ardwick. We found that an overnight transit was regularly achievable via Heysham, Leeds Stourton and Derby St Marys, which on a map looks a very long way round. The secret was, of course, that each leg of the rail journey had been planned long ago for fast transits, and the marshalling yards had a simple shunt to take off the shipping traffic from the front of the incoming train and put it on the front of the forward train, which would then be on its way very quickly. At Derby the BD would be on the rear to Manchester, the first to be shunted under the crane on arrival. The 'direct' Heysham to Manchester via Preston route took three days.

The forwarding of ISO containers was increasing, as was the loading of ferry vans from the Inland Port. We loaded 20ft Freightliner containers on 40ft wagons. Camden Goods Depot and Landor Street could each load two containers to Belfast and two to Dublin. The wagons were marshalled at Exchange Sidings, Birmingham, and the Dublin containers were detached at Crewe. We lifted ISO containers with single point lift cranes, which made it difficult if the weight was not evenly distributed. When 30ft containers arrived, Doncaster Works fabricated a special adjustable spreader for single lift cranes. This was a mite cumbersome but worked well with unevenly weighted loads.

Our gantry crane at Lawley Street spanned two rail sidings with a roadway in between. It was a rail-mounted Goliath crane which the Outdoor Machinery Department kept running reliably. We hired a BRS lorry and trombone trailer to deliver masses of reinforcing rods for building the M6. Their cheerful driver had only one eye, yet he safely delivered many loads through the back streets.

Wagon load services had been adopted or developed to move ISO containers overnight between Landor Street and Liverpool Canada Dock, Hull, Southampton, and Kings Lynn. Other ports were sometimes served. ISO Platefits (with the wooden bodies removed) were restricted to Liverpool. ISO Lowmacs, with a steel angle carrying frame for the ISO container mounted on them, were able to pass freely over the system. The problem with the Lowmacs was breakage of suspension eye-bolts, strained when containers were dropped onto the wagon. We had a very good Carriage & Wagon man who shot off in a road van to repair wagons around the district and get them on their way. Maintaining an overnight transit was very important indeed, and Landor Street had earned a good reputation for reliable transits.

At Landor Street one morning some drivers reported for duty and saw to their horror that five ISO containers, which they had loaded for despatch to Kings Lynn Docks the previous evening, were still standing under the gantry crane. The late turn shunter must only have drawn out the wagons standing on the front road and cannot have checked the labels on the five wagons on the back road.

Realising the vital importance of connecting the ISO containers with the weekly sailing that evening on the MV *Alster* from Kings Lynn to Hamburg, on which spaces had been booked for later that day, the drivers reloaded with the help of the crane driver and were soon driving out into Landor Street, before anyone else arrived. Three of their vehicles were what we then called 21-ton tractors with ISO-frame trailers and two were Scammell–coupling 8- or 12-ton units with flat bed trailers. Each trailer had a 20ft container securely loaded and the lead driver, Colin Hunt, had made sure he had picked up the shipping papers.

The convoy headed for Kings Lynn Docks and were able to position their containers alongside the vessels ready to be craned aboard. The men drove back via Leicester Goods Depot, to refuel, and on to Birmingham to receive a warm welcome at Landor Street. They continued to give excellent service with Birmingham Inland Port and later Freightliners Ltd.

Even, as here, with the 1960s best in cranes and wagons, positioning a container on the wagon twistlocks called for considerable care and skill. With a single point lift crane the task was even more exacting

Editor's note: This reminded me of the efforts we made in the London Suburban district to move perishable and vulnerable traffic during the 1955 ASLEF strike. My cartage and terminals section had two excellent inspectors, Dick Hayden and Dave McPhee, and a brilliant and highly versatile team of motor and crane drivers. One of the former, Vic Groves, even took a load all the way from London to Edinburgh using his 3-ton, three-wheeled articulated unit and trailer. Three hundred miles each way with a three-wheeler! On another occasion one of the mobile crane drivers tackled the delicate task of lifting fragile Roman remains as part of archaeological excavation.

Two Royal Journeys

Being in charge on a royal train journey was quite a responsibility with a constant risk of the unexpected, as these accounts by John Ellis and Bill Parker show.

Outward Journey

John Ellis records: 'When I was divisional manager at Liverpool Street in the early '80s, the Queen and Prince Philip were booked to go by train to a series of engagements in Cambridge. Because of the problems of getting a royal train into any London terminal during the morning rush hour, it was decided to take the royal party on the 09.35 service train from Liverpool Street. I was chosen as train manager, my first experience of this responsibility.

There were considerable problems in managing the security arrangements in the station at the peak of the morning rush hour, and there was a fair amount of delay to trains arriving, and disruption on the concourses (this was before Liverpool Street had been redeveloped and remodelled), but the 09.35 started only a few minutes late.

As we travelled north, the train slowed and then came to a halt. This was before the days of mobile phones so it was difficult to establish the cause of delay, except via the BT police radio phone. It transpired that the previous train had been stopped out of course at Harlow, at the insistence of a peer who was due to be greeting the royal party at Cambridge, and who had missed the scheduled train. The discussions and consultation about a special stop order for the train took a long time, and created the delay to the 09.35.

The schedule for the day was busy and tight, and a late arrival would create a lot of difficulties. I was summoned to explain the position to the Duke of Edinburgh, and received the sharp end of his tongue for the delay!

It was my first, and last, time as train manager for a royal party!'

Return

The same occasion was Bill Parker's last time in charge of a royal journey but he had rather better fortune, remembering: 'I was in the line up for the arrival of the royal party at Cambridge station, dressed in my best and accompanied by Barbara, my wife, in an expensive new dress. There were the usual courtesies but, understandably, everything was much hurried and somewhat lacking in the customary broad smiles, all of which did not bode well for my return journey in charge.

On the way back in the evening, as we passed the area where the delay had occurred earlier, an equerry came into my apartment with a summons to come to Her Majesty. I wondered if the matter of the morning delays was going to resurface and was in a right sweat as we walked together to obey, especially as the equerry declined, albeit in a really charming manner, to disclose the reason for the summons. I feared the worst but, happily, it turned out so much better than I had expected. My apprehension quickly evaporated during a most pleasant discussion about my earlier association with royal journeys and my impending retirement. However, the Duke did express the hope that the train would not be late at Liverpool Street!'

Well Caught

Among many unusual incidents which civil engineer Jim Dorward came across in his career was this one at Barrhead where two wrongs did make something of a right.

When Barrhead was being resignalled in the early 1970s there was a spell of a few days when movements into and out of the Down bay platform where being controlled by hand signalmen. During this period catch points on the Up line north of Barrhead were found to be sitting slightly open on the morning of the Friday prior to their removal on the following Sunday. As their removal was imminent it was decided not to arrange their adjustment, bearing in mind that catch points were very rarely used in anger.

As a result of a misunderstanding between the signalman and a hand signalman on that Friday afternoon, a three-car diesel multiple unit departing from the bay platform for Glasgow was routed onto the Up line as a result of a crossover not having been reset after the train's earlier arrival from Glasgow. Surprisingly, the driver of the departing train did not notice that he negotiated the crossover and was now proceeding on the wrong line.

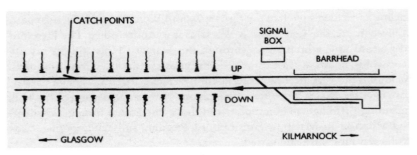

Catch points in the open position as a protection against a runaway.

After some 400 yards the train approached the catch points which were sitting slightly open. The left-hand wheels of the leading bogie managed to pass between the slightly open switch rail and the stock rail, but the movement made the switch rails close to the proper position resulting in the remainder of the train being derailed. Mercifully as a result of the leading bogie remaining on the track the train was probably saved from tumbling down the steep embankment.

This was one of those very rare occasions when a track defect proved a blessing in disguise by preventing the possibility of a more serious accident had the dmu continued on the wrong line.

Worcester

Ian Body enjoyed his time as assistant area manager at Worcester, but it was not without incident.

The Worcester area manager's patch was a very varied one controlling both the section of the Bristol-Birmingham main line which included the Lickey

Incline and a long stretch of the former Oxford, Worcester & Wolverhampton Railway route, the 'Old Worse & Worse' as it was once called. The Hereford to Oxford line, which passes through the Malvern Hills and on via the Cotswolds, boasts at least three resident ghosts and a selection of tunnels, including the very narrow Colwall Tunnel. There has always been a lot of passenger business at Worcester's two stations, Foregate Street and Shrub Hill, including Birmingham commuters and those east-bound through Evesham and Moreton-in-Marsh towards Oxford, Reading and Paddington. Goods traffic was substantial and varied.

From time to time a consignment of Seville oranges would arrive in the goods yard at Shrub Hill in Transfesa wagons. The fine, colourful fruit was packed in the traditional, wire-bound boxes which had to be unloaded manually from wagon to delivery vehicle. On one occasion the first of two wagons was opened and unloaded without any problems and one of the yard staff duly moved on to pull back the doors of the next vehicle. It must have been an off day in Spain when that vehicle was loaded for although the oranges were all there they had not been boxed and one astonished railwayman was swept off his feet by an unstoppable tide of loose oranges!

Drama of a different kind occurred along on the line to Hereford. There a late turn signalman at one of the remote signal boxes was minding his own business on what had been an unremarkable shift. There were no trains about, it was pitch dark outside and he was experiencing that sense of total isolation and quiet that country signalmen knew well. Until, that is, a tiny sound caught his attention. Nothing dramatic but, from long experience, he identified it as the movement of a signal wire. Something or someone had brushed against it in the darkness. Nothing very unusual about that; must be an animal he thought, until the door of his dimly lit box was suddenly flung open with a crash that shattered the peace of the night. A group of burly figures burst in, shouting and ferocious and quickly seized the astonished signalman, gagged him and tied him securely to his own chair. Their leader then promptly reported the capture over his walkie-talkie and assumed the smug expression of a job well done. Indeed it was so far as the Territorial Army was concerned. Their night exercise had been carried out without a hitch and their objective had been achieved.

When the much-shaken signalman was finally released and had explained the enormity of the TA's action in graphic detail, their self-satisfaction quickly wilted. Someone was going to suffer from the inevitable official retribution!

Of course, there were many lighter moments, one of these concerning the neighbouring Gloucester area. As part of the mild rivalry between the two, Bernard Whitaker at Worcester prepared an official-looking letter, which he duly addressed to his colleague and friend John Jones who was area manager at Gloucester. It purported to come from the railway's regional fire chief and offered Gloucester the privilege of a 'controlled conflagration' to test the response of the area staff. To have declined the offer would have appeared insensitive to the importance of being well prepared for the possibility of fire, so John accepted.

The next letter offered Gloucester the choice of the size of fire to be provided, small, medium or large. Small would have suggested lack of commitment but large seemed altogether too dramatic. Medium was chosen and brought a request for choice of location. John could not think of anywhere a medium fire might not precipitate all manner of problems. By now he was decidedly nervous about the whole situation and where matters might finish up. Bernard, too, could see that the whole prank was gaining too much momentum of its own. He decided that he had to be the first to weaken and duly confessed his guilt. There were no hard feelings.

Ian also records another unusual occurrence at Worcester in the following words: 'It was a warm, quiet afternoon at Shrub Hill and I was making my way along the main platform towards the bay at the north end where there was a short train made up of three GUV parcels vans with a locomotive attached. This was not a regular working so I naturally enquired of the supervisor as to its destination and departure time.

The response was rather surprising. Apparently the train was destined for Derby and was somewhat late for a reason that was decidedly unusual. It appeared that one van contained a coffin and its occupant, and also that the driver was very clear that he was not prepared to work the train forward unless the 'occupant' was travelling in what he considered to be the right direction. He was adamant that, as he put it, 'We leave this world feet first' and that either the coffin or the train had to be turned to achieve this.

My first assumption was that the driver was surely joking but it quickly became clear that his view was absolute with no room for manoeuvre or persuasion. The mood also appeared to be contagious for the platform staff promptly either miraculously disappeared or suddenly had other pressing work which had to be addressed. Thus the option of turning the coffin itself dropped off the list.

To save any further delay and the questions from Bristol Control which could prove hard to answer, I decided to turn the train which duly set off towards Foregate Street and then back into Shrub Hill via Tunnel Junction. After 45 minutes' delay the train's only passenger was then able to make his or her way out of Worcester for the last time, comfortingly leaving both the station and this world in the right direction!

The thought of trying to discipline the traincrew and getting involved in a debate about obscure religious doctrine seemed uninviting, especially with the parallel risk of the media headlining inventive versions of the railway Conditions of Carriage. I decided that the incident was best just put down to experience.'

Vancos

At Doncaster one of Bill Parker's responsibilities was that of making arrangements for the carriage of dead people by train.

Coming straight from National Service and as a clerk in the passenger trains office of the Doncaster district superintendent, I learned about, and was greatly surprised by, the extent of the railway involvement in moving corpses by train. This was done under special arrangements laid down to ensure great sensitivity and proper, respectful treatment.

The initial contact, usually from an undertaker, was to the district passenger manager's office who dealt with the commercial and financial aspects, with the matter then coming to me to arrange the actual movement. It was my job to organise the provision of a suitable vehicle, generally a fitted freight van or a passenger guard's van depending on the type of train involved, and then plan its journey based on a predetermined list of approved services. The process of advising everyone at the destination and en route was all done under the telegraph code word 'Vanco'.

Quite often mourners travelled in accommodation on the same train as the coffin. As a mark of respect the local station master or a suitable representative would normally be in attendance at the starting and destination stations. I encountered such occasions myself as a summer relief station master and found the experience of receiving a Vanco quite moving.

My Vanco workload was no more than half a dozen or so cases a month but each movement was treated seriously and I am pleased to reflect that we never lost or mislaid one body during the two winter periods I was in the office. The same could not be said for the mourners who sometimes exhibited a bewildering inclination to wander off on their own and in the wrong direction.

Much later on, as divisional manager at Kings Cross, I learned about the funeral train station in the Kings Cross area from which trains carrying coffins and mourners ran to Southgate cemetery in the nineteenth century. Train paths were included in the timetable and a special scale of charges was laid down.

One of the potential sites had been the Kings Cross goods yard which I knew in the 1950s as a district inspector and from my goods depot training as a traffic apprentice. Then it was very busy with freight full loads and sundries plus priority traffics like the important fish trains from Scotland, and the comings and goings of numerous road cartage vehicles. I found it interesting to reflect on how the funeral station, its trains and mourners would have fitted in with the noise, smells and activity of the area in the nineteenth century. The other potential site had been alongside the passenger station.

At one time the movement of bodies for burial was big business for two of the London rail terminals, Waterloo and Kings Cross. Both had separate and elaborate funeral stations, this faded photograph showing the Kings Cross one, from which funeral trains carried the deceased and their mourners to the cemetery at Southgate. (Revd Martin Dawes)

The funeral station was, however, built on the east side of the main line, to the north of Gasworks Tunnel.

The original Kings Cross funeral train activity has been thoroughly researched and documented by the Revd Martin Dawes in his informative and fascinating book *The End of the Line*. This also resolved for me a long-standing mystery of how a former signal box near New Southgate got its name. The Cemetery box used to control access to and from the long siding into the cemetery there.

Bounds Green and the Specials

John Cronin describes a period at the Bounds Green coaching stock maintenance depot when the spirit of Christmas led to a remarkable event with some unexpected consequences.

Bounds Green depot is located on the Up side of the East Coast Main Line, just north of Alexandra Palace station some 5 miles from London Kings Cross. It was originally built as a repair depot for locomotive-hauled carriages to deal mainly with the lifting and wheel set change activities that otherwise would have required a defective vehicle being sent to Doncaster Carriage Works. In the early 1970s the depot was considerably enhanced with the provision of a six-road train shed with inspection pits and cleaning platforms, in preparation for the arrival of the first of the production series of InterCity 125 High Speed Trains due to enter service on the East Coast route in 1976. These new facilities also meant that the residual loco-hauled coaching stock servicing and maintenance could be brought together under one roof and so eliminate the 'fresh air engineering' maintenance that had been previously carried out in open carriage sidings at Holloway, Hornsey and Bounds Green.

From 1974 onwards I watched the development of Bounds Green from just up the road at Hornsey where I was the area maintenance engineer charged with setting up and commissioning the new Electric Multiple Unit Maintenance Depot and the Great Northern Suburban 25kv Overhead Line Fixed Equipment system ready to introduce the Class 313 dual voltage inner suburban units in 1975/76 and the Class 312 single voltage outer suburban units in 1978. To make this happen we had to recruit over 200 people of various skills, all new to the railway industry, whom we then had to train and mould into a team; but that is a story in its own right.

At Bounds Green in the summer of 1979 the resident depot manager, David Perry, was seconded for six months to work with Transmark, the British Railways consultancy division, in Canada. To cover for David's absence I was invited to move a mile down the road to see whether I could work a little bit of the 'Cronin Magic', as my boss so eloquently put it, on an older, established depot team, a challenge that he knew I could not refuse. Six months on in early 1980 David Perry decided Canada was his future and so for me what had started as a six-month secondment now became a permanent appointment.

Over the next nine years we were to see many changes at Bounds Green as the day and overnight loco-hauled services were slowly phased out on the East Coast route as more High Speed Trains became available and the postal and parcel train business became just a memory. During the latter years of the decade we prepared the depot for the arrival of the Class 91 electric locomotives and the InterCity225 MK 4 coaches.

But let us go back to the early years of the decade when overnight services were still provided by MK1 sleeping cars supported by MK2 D, E & F air-conditioned day coaches. The sleeping cars were by then looking very tired and the facilities offered to customers and on board staff were judged to be very poor in comparison with what we offered on long-distance daytime InterCity services. This fact had been recognised back in the 1970s when a design for a MK3 sleeping car was developed following the successful introduction into service of MK3 coaches in both traditional loco-hauled and InterCity125 HST modes. The proposed MK3 sleeping cars incorporated all the main MK3 features of air conditioning, improved insulation and good riding and were at the detailed design stage when, early on a July morning in 1978, twelve passengers died at Taunton in a fire on a MK1 sleeping car train from Penzance to London. This tragic event delayed the MK3 design process by many months and eventually resulted in modifications to include much greater fire resistance.

For Bounds Green this delay meant we had to keep the MK1 sleeping cars in service for longer than planned, an extra challenge we could well have done without as HST performance in the same period continued to be poor in terms of both availability and reliability. Thus, in the autumn of 1982, when the first of the new MK3 sleeping cars started to arrive at the depot for commissioning, I thought, at last, we would see the light at the end of the tunnel so far as our overnight service problems were concerned.

This now brings me to a novel story about the press launch for the new MK3 sleepers that the InterCity business planned to stage between London Kings Cross and Edinburgh Waverley in the period between Christmas and New Year in 1982. In the last days before Christmas we had received just enough new MK3 sleepers to, in theory, form two East Coast sleeping car train sets, but in reality we had just sufficient commissioned to form the Press Launch Special.

The set for the special was ready by Christmas Eve and stood in the shed alongside a rake of MK1 sleepers that we had put together to form another special to Aberdeen to collect the children from the Rudolph Steiner School and bring them home to their parents and families in the south after they had celebrated Christmas with their friends at the school. Those children are severely disabled in many ways and this particular train has always been dear to the heart of many of the Bounds Green team who year on year have volunteered to travel north to welcome the children on board at Aberdeen and provide support to the children and their helpers on the long journey south.

On that Christmas Eve I remained on duty with the team as we closed the railway down for Christmas and, during the evening as we waited for the incoming HST fleet for servicing, it was suggested that I might like to look through the two sleeping car sets whilst they remained in the shed. Good idea, I thought, and off we went, first through the gleaming new set and then back through the elderly, tired and worn MK1 'Rudolph Steiner' set. Back on the shed floor we stood and looked at the two sets and I suddenly realised how quiet the normally noisy diesel depot had become. As I looked around to see why, I noticed small groups of staff standing in the shadows silently watching. Of course it was plain for all to see that there was no comparison between the two trains and I felt deeply ashamed at what we proposed to send to bring those wonderful children home. In truth those MK1 sleepers were only fit for the scrapyard and I must admit I felt like a certain 'Mr Scrooge' as we stood there in the shed and heard the church bells ring.

The spirit of Christmas was in the air and the decision was taken 'to fail the MK1 set for technical reasons' and step up the MK3 press set to work the 'Rudolph Steiner'. Thankfully the senior managers at the various levels must have all left work for home by this early hour on Christmas morning so there was no one readily available to advise on our plan. As well as the volunteer cleaners, over a cup of tea in the production office, two technical inspectors and a production manager offered to go with the train as they were mindful that the MK3 sleepers had run only a few miles to date, of which none were with passengers, so the 'Rudolph Steiner' would provide us with an 'in service trial' before the press launch scheduled to run just 48 hours later.

Christmas was spent at my home with Mum in Potters Bar and late on Boxing Day evening I said good night to her and left to drive to the depot to be on hand to see the 'Rudolph Steiner' leave for the North via Bowes Park and the Hertford North branch.

The train, headed by a specially cleaned long-range Class 47/4 diesel locomotive, emerged from the shed into a crisp, cloudless, moonlit night and slowly climbed out of the depot yard and under the bridge to join the Hertford North branch for the start of the long journey to Aberdeen. As the taillight disappeared under the bridge it was time to get the HSTs ready for service later in the morning and it wasn't until I was sure that the 'Rudolph Steiner' was well on her way to Scotland that I rang York Regional Control and advised them of the decisions taken. 'Be it on your head Mr Cronin,' was my good friend the chief controller's response. 'I might mention your call if anyone asks about the 'Steiner' but keep your fingers crossed that no one does. Now what about your High Speed Trains? Can I hope for a good service from you this morning?'

The hours passed and night turned to day and I was home again when the call came to tell me the train had arrived safely in Aberdeen, and the depot volunteers had been overwhelmed by the reception they received when the children and their helpers and many parents saw our super brand new train that had come to collect them. The journey south that evening went like a dream as the word got about amongst the 'Railway Family' and it was green lights all the way as the 'Rudolph Steiner' became a 'Royal' in all but name.

Technology in those days was still steam-age compared to the world we live in today, but somehow the BBC found out about our train and it appeared on their national early evening TV news. As you might guess my bosses saw the news item and soon the telephone was ringing seeking explanations, regardless of the good publicity it was for the railway industry. By then, of course, the train was safely back in the depot at Bounds Green and we were already well on the way to preparing her, once again, for the Press Launch Special due to run the next evening.

What the 'in service trial' had highlighted were problems with the new coach boilers. Three had failed during the trip to Scotland and we needed to adjust all the air-conditioning systems as the coach interior temperatures were too high.

The next evening saw the press people descend on the train in numbers as it was 'news' and many enjoyed copious nightcaps before retiring to their bunks long after midnight, looking forward to a good night's sleep before a full Scottish breakfast in the North British Hotel on arrival in Edinburgh. I am pleased to report the launch was judged a great success by all and nothing more was said about 'The Steiner Affair'.

At the depot the team were elated by our success, and it got 1983 off to the flying start that we needed as the reliability of our HSTs continued to generate serious problems that were mainly out of our control to resolve in the short term.

A Sequel

This episode led to a working relationship with David Ward of InterCity Special Trains that resulted in Bounds Green depot becoming the home of InterCity Charters, and also with the immensely likeable Bernard Staite, the Steam Locomotive Owners Association's operations manager. It started later in 1983 with the arrival at the depot of the SLOA MK1 Met-Cam Pullman set to be prepared as a one-off for a return to the East Coast Main Line of steam traction in the form of LNER Class A3 Pacific No.4472 *Flying Scotsman*. To provide First Class dining we needed a full MK1 Kitchen Car and Ray Loft, InterCity resources manager, kindly arranged the temporary transfer of RKB No.1513 from the West Coast. The vehicle looked like new in her BR corporate blue and grey livery, as she had been fully restored in 1982 to run in the 100th Anniversary On Train Dining Special that toured the railway as a mobile exhibition and corporate hospitality train. On the day all went well with the steam run, the whole of the East Coast route being lined with sightseers from Peterborough North to York.

Following that event it was agreed the Pullman set could transfer from her base at Carlisle to Bounds Green as long as it did not detract from the total commitment required of the depot team to keep the High Speed Trains running despite their ongoing problems.

As our reputation for a quality product grew, more vehicles were acquired to meet a growing demand for First Class charter trains, all with full dining

InterCity MK1 charter train coach with the trademark 'Bounds Green White Roof'. (John Cronin Collection)

facilities and, with the introduction of the 'Swallow' livery, the famous Bounds Green white coach roofs appeared to compliment the new livery.

Through this exciting period the SLOA Pullman set became the mainstay of the public steam-hauled charter trains, including the Sunday Luncheon Trains from London Marylebone to Stratford-on-Avon, that saw many famous express steam locomotives used, and on one famous occasion we had the choice of two Class A4's plus *Flying Scotsman* to work two dining trains.

We also celebrated the fiftieth anniversary of the naming of Class A4 Pacific No.4498 *Sir Nigel Gresley* at Marylebone Station on 26 November 1937 by William Whitelaw, a director of the LNER. For the anniversary on Thursday 26 November 1987 Bounds Green provided three MK1 first class vehicles to 'Royal' standard to convey the A4 Locomotive Society chairman and his guests from Marylebone to Gerrards Cross for their anniversary dinner. The train was worked from Bounds Green by Old Oak Common InterCity Class 47/8 No.47841 recently named *The Institution of Mechanical Engineers* and the whole train looked a picture as she slowly rolled into a dimly lit Marylebone station.

Then, on a Saturday in May 1988, Bounds Green provided two MK1 InterCity Charter sets and an InterCity 125 HST for a BBC celebration of the lives of John and Charles Wesley, the founders of the Methodist Church. In recognition of the lives of these two men Power Car No.43103 was named *John Wesley* and No.43114 *Charles Wesley* at St Pancras station, before over 1,000 Methodists sang the first hymn of many that day, *Oh for a Thousand Tongues to Sing*, to the surprise of hundreds of English and Scottish football fans on their way to Wembley for what proved to be the last International between the two countries for many a year.

Later that summer, on a Sunday in July, we celebrated the fiftieth anniversary of LNER Class A4 Pacific No.4468 *Mallard* breaking the world steam traction speed record. The original plan was to use a new Class 91 electric locomotive to haul the Bounds Green designated Charter VIP set of MK1 coaches from London Kings Cross to Doncaster where the electric would give way to No.4468 for the onward journey to York. Sadly at the time the early Class 91 locomotive performance was poor and so the depot provided Class 89 No.89001 *Badger* to do the job. There was a contractual dispute going on so the depot was not allowed to repaint the locomotive as we would have wished, other than the buffer beam that we repainted in keeping with the East Coast tradition with the locomotive number and home depot name 'Bounds Green'.

Then in March 1989 it was all over for me so far as Bounds Green depot was concerned as I set off for Bristol and the Great Western to face new challenges, taking with me great pride in what we, the 'Bounds Green Team', had together achieved and so many happy memories of which I have described just a few.

Staff family-dedication service at Bounds Green, with John Cronin in front of No.43057 *Bounds Green* and flanked by InterCity Director John Prideaux and railway chaplain Alan Cook. (John Cronin Collection)

A Paddle in Gas Works Tunnel

Dealing with the unexpected is part of railway life, as area manager Kings Cross, Charles Wort, knew only too well.

One morning in 1982, during a very heavy rain storm, Gas Works Tunnel on the approaches to Kings Cross became flooded by over 2ft of water. There was also flooding to a lesser extent in the large area between the tunnel and the station platforms known as 'The Throat'.

Initially the depth and extent of the flooding was not known but the situation was clearly serious enough to terminate all passenger services at Finsbury Park. As this decision was being implemented through the divisional control office, key members of the divisional and area manager's staff were sent to Finsbury Park to deal with the many aspects of terminating and starting main line trains there. In addition to the operational considerations, the team needed to keep passengers informed and help them to transfer between main line and underground services and to make use of the local and additional, hastily organised, LT bus services.

Charles Wort and his operations manager Charles Wells considered the water was coming from Kings Cross goods yard. They, nonetheless, decided to enter the tunnel to try to pin down the exact source, whether it was coming from the roof or below ground. As the former recalls, the two were dressed rather like unusually quaint divers in uncomfortable high waders, vast waterproof capes, bowler hats and carrying mini-searchlights. Quite soon they were left in no doubt about where the immediate water flow was coming from and this was accompanied by the realisation that they should have been wearing steel helmets, for their bowlers were no protection against the streaming water which rained down over the brims of their hats, over their faces and then down their necks! Their experience was not improved by having to wade through 'very deep water on an invisible, rough track formation'.

The divisional civil engineer's staff were also on the scene and the cause of the flooding was found to be the inadequacy of the drains to cope with the heavy and continuing rainfall. It was several hours later and well into the afternoon before the pumps and drains were able to clear the water and the divisional signal engineer's men could repair the ground-level signalling equipment. At last the job was completed and train services could be returned to Kings Cross.

As Charles Wort recalls, he and Charles Wells felt that they looked like 'a couple of real Charlies' as they made their journey into the unknown darkness of the flooded tunnel.

Summer in Fenland and West Norfolk

For two summers during his first managerial appointment after traffic apprentice training, Bill Parker, as general assistant to the traffic manager at Cambridge, had the job of supervising most of the summer weekend peak workings in Fenland and West Norfolk.

One of the summer highlights of operations in the Cambridge operating district was the weekend booked and excursion special passenger trains which passed through from the East and West Midlands, Yorkshire and further north via Peterborough or the GE/GN Joint line and on to the East Anglian seaside resorts, such as Hunstanton, Cromer, Sheringham, Great Yarmouth and Lowestoft.

They were through trains insofar as they did not stop at stations in the Cambridge district, apart from some of the seaside stations between Kings Lynn and the terminus at Hunstanton, but the majority had to make a stop to change engines at the signal boxes in the March station area, due to engineering-imposed route restrictions in East Anglia for certain classes of engines. These boxes were the focal points of the summer weekend train operation, along with Whitemoor Junction signal box which controlled access to and from March engine shed.

Over each weekend several dozen passenger trains required an engine change at March on the outward and return journeys. The hard core of the

Saturday-only holiday passenger trains were in the main timetable, with a few additional trains planned on special circulars, whereas the majority of the Sunday excursions were planned by special circulars. Separate engine and train crew diagrams and rosters had to be issued for each weekend's operations. By this time the former M&GN weekend summer services via South Lynn and Melton Constable had been rerouted via March.

The engine change at the March signal boxes was allocated only a very few minutes; I recall the maximum time was four. This demanded very slick movements by the train crews, the signalmen and shunters, and in the light engine movements to and from the depot. Everyone had a key part to play in the process. With so many trains, the timing and train pathing was inevitably tight, and late running sometimes caused bunching and additional delays. This put extra pressure on the shunting and engine shed staff to avoid any further delays and created the need to adjust the footplate and guard allocations.

Despite the considerably increased passenger train activity, a re-planned weekend freight train service also operated although on a smaller scale than normal. The arrangements which had to be made, including determining priorities and overseeing the working of the Whitemoor marshalling yards, were in the capable hands of the yard master, Harry Onyon, who liaised with Whitemoor Junction signal box and Cambridge district control office.

I was given a short briefing for my role in charge by traffic manager Alan Suddaby, operating superintendent Harry Crosthwaite and his assistant the inimitable George Docking, and motive power superintendent Geoff Parslew. I recall George concluding the meeting with the words, 'It will mean long and tough days for you, lad,' adding, with a broad smile on his face which gave me some comfort, 'but it will do you good!'

I was to be supported at ground level by a very experienced and efficient team, most of whom had done it all many times before. At March were district inspectors Henry Orbell and Percy Baynes; a senior assistant from the district passenger trains section; March station master Cyril Tunn; Whitemoor yard master Harry Onyon and March shed master Geoff Liversedge and his running and mechanical foremen, the latter with the heavy breakdown crane in steam. At Kings Lynn were district inspector Stan Simpson, on loan from Cambridge, who was also in charge of the regulation of trains over the Hunstanton branch; Kings Lynn station master Billy Hill and shed master Ted Shaw, and his running and mechanical foremen, also with their crane in steam. District inspector Jimmy Greaves was at Hunstanton, along with station master Walter Westley with his floral button hole, and his station foreman Billy Brunning. The latter's speciality was moving empty rolling stock to Heacham and propelling them into the sidings there when Hunstanton carriage sidings were full. A running and mechanical foreman and fitters from the Kings Lynn shed were also on hand.

Senior staff from Cambridge paid regular visits to cheer on the troops, and the permanent way, signalling and carriage and wagon people all made their contribution.

The BT police were assisted by some strapping fellows from the Cambridgeshire and Norfolk constabularies, all well versed in crowd control. Hosts of other staff, from shunters to cleaners and office staff, all made their contribution, and we had special telephone links to all important locations. What could possible go wrong? I was confident, but not complacent. All these professionals knew what to expect – and so did I after the first weekend!

Despite the vast amount of activity in the weeks of summer, I remember those Saturdays and Sundays as an example of excellent teamwork, with good pre-planning (brainwork, paper and pencil – no computers in those days), first class execution, with quick, practical and effective decisions to change the plan as circumstances demanded (and most of the time it did) and executed by dedicated, hard working, practical railwaymen of all grades.

Not everything went to plan, of course. Common to many days was the late running, often very late, of the incoming passenger trains. This threw the planned engine and train crew diagrams and rosters completely out of phase, and gave the shed foremen and train crew signing-on staff at March and Kings Lynn severe problems in having to constantly reschedule and reallocate engines and crews. They, strongly supported by the district passenger trains assistant whose prime task was to develop temporary diagrams and rosters, barely had a minute to spare such was their personal active involvement in keeping the job going. Ted Shaw, particularly, was noted for his general distrust in the Great Eastern line manager's Shenfield HQ office diagrams. He considered them impracticable, especially on summer weekends, because of the inevitable late running. Accordingly he worked the engines and crews on the branch on an ad hoc basis, and extremely well too.

The shunting staff, however constantly and hard they tried, were not able on many occasions to achieve the scheduled engine changing time, again because of the late running which put their plans out of gear by having to wait for fresh engines, or two trains on site instead of one. They also had to cope with couplings that were unnaturally stiff and there were problems in creating the vacuum brake in what was often relatively little-used rolling stock. With the help of train crews and C&W fitters, and by pulling the strings in the vacuum braking procedure, most of the difficulties were overcome but not without compounding the already late services.

Over each summer there would be at least a couple of minor derailments in the sheds; and although promptly dealt with by using an alternative route for the engine movements, these incidents compounded the already busy shed activities. The occasional points, signals or track circuit failures also got prompt treatment but added to train delays.

Ray Unwin's copy of a photograph taken at the retirement of district inspector Jimmy Greaves. In the centre of the front row Jimmy has George Docking on his right and Harry Crosthwaithe on his left, with the Hunstanton, Kings Lynn and Heacham station masters beyond. Those behind also played a major part in the Cambridge district's fruit season and summer special train operations and include chief district inspector Cyril Rose, and district inspectors Stan Simpson, Percy Baynes and Ray himself.

As could be expected with thousands of passengers of all ages, generations and physical abilities there were numerous occasions when medical or other travel help was needed. This was given at the main stations, i.e. March, Kings Lynn and sometimes at Ely, where we usually had railway first-aiders on duty or stand-by ambulances and medical staff.

The presence of so many 'foreign' engines represented a paradise for trainspotters, who lined the route, especially near March station level crossing gates and in the playing field opposite March West Junction signal box. Quite a few were also permitted onto March station platforms, Cyril Tunn and his staff ensuring they bought a platform ticket! The policemen were invaluable in crowd control and had an active role in keeping the trainspotters from letting their enthusiasm result in trespass or danger. Some spotters actually got into the loco depot but I do not recall any arrests and the whole question was treated sensitively and with an eye on public relations.

The layout at Kings Lynn required the passenger trains to come into the station platforms in order to get the fresh engine on the rear. Inevitably this caused a situation whereby some passengers got off their train and made a dash for the toilets or the nearby pub. Happily, the policemen had a restraining influence but, even so, the station staff had no mean task in getting everyone back on board, except by using the then modern technology – the loudhailer – and by a mixture of shouting, using whistles and by sheer force of personality.

Hunstanton station was a hive of activity. Up to 1,000 passengers at a time had to be shepherded between trains, platforms and the conveniently large space just outside the station. Mums and dads, with families including toddlers, babies in prams and pushchairs, older relations and handicapped people in wheelchairs – almost everyone with lots of luggage – all take some handling, especially in persuading them to hurry. After all, they were in holiday mood, but Walter Westley did wonders with his loudhailer!

Despite the crowds, mishaps to passengers were few and far between and usually involved people slipping or falling over other passengers' cases in the general hustle and bustle. First-aiders quickly took over and soon got the passengers on their way. Nonetheless there was an occasion when a youth fell onto the track. His injuries were serious with concussion and several fractures. The ambulance crew was quickly on the scene, but obviously there was a fairly long hold-up in getting the track clear.

One very sad and worrying occasion occurred when an elderly lady passenger had collapsed and died as her train was nearing Hunstanton. This incident clearly caused a problem as the policemen on the platform took over until the ambulance crew arrived at the compartment, the station master comforting her relatives until they and the deceased were taken away by ambulance. Fortunately the policemen did not declare it to be a crime site, and it was not too long before the empty train was released and moved to the carriage sidings.

One of the problems at Hunstanton, and to a lesser extent at Kings Lynn, was the vast amount of rubbish left on the platforms and thrown onto the track by the passengers. Despite the intense platform occupation by trains, the station cleaning staff and platelayers worked like Trojans between trains to clear up as much mess as possible. Another unfortunate factor was the use of, and pulling the chain in, the toilets when the trains were stationary at those stations. The platelayers did their best to overcome the 'residual problem'. The limited opportunities between trains and the crowds to clean up also meant a long period of work later to undertake a heavy clean of the whole of the station area.

The team of carriage cleaners had the unenviable job of clearing what were very dirty train interiors quickly and the carriage and wagon staff were kept busy undertaking repairs to seats, sliding and toilet doors, and to the undercarriages.

Passengers for the outgoing trains were managed by controlled queuing outside the station buildings and this was generally acceptable unless it was raining. On a few wet occasions their irritation might have led to nasty incidents had it not been for the excellent police presence. Otherwise, the behaviour of the several thousand passengers was very good, the occasional exception being when too much alcohol had been taken, resulting in drunken, mildly aggressive, violent and abusive behaviour. Such miscreants were arrested by the Norfolk Constabulary policemen and spent a night in the Kings Lynn cells.

The local publican near March station did very well out of these busy weekends, although we railwaymen had only time to send a messenger to the BR Staff Association club for what we could consume on the job. Sweet tea from the signal box helped, as did the occasional meal of fish and chips in newspaper at Hunstanton and the well-earned pints of beer from the Sandringham Hotel there.

Much has changed over the years but George Docking's observations were so right. These were indeed very long days and extremely hard and tiring work, but they certainly did me a lot of good. I learned much about effective cooperation and coordination and how to cope with what seemed to be a constant stream of unending problems. They were also, nonetheless, most satisfying and enjoyable to all of us dedicated railwaymen, and gave us the great satisfaction of helping thousands of holidaymakers and trippers on their seaside journeys.

A Coupling and a Breakfast

David Ward tells of two very different incidents involving a royal train.

The buckeye coupling used on corridor carriages and parcels vans was standard for many years on the Southern and London & North Eastern Railways, and became the standard coupling on BR corridor carriages and vans from 1950. This buckeye coupling was considered much safer than the linked screw coupling used by the London Midland & Scottish Railway and the Great Western because in a derailment it could be generally relied upon to keep the carriages coupled together and upright and thus minimise damage and injury to passengers. It was also safer for shunters because they only needed to go between carriages to couple brake and other hoses after vehicles were firmly coupled together.

To enable a buckeye coupling carriage to be attached to a screw-coupled carriage it was necessary for the coupling to be hinged so that it could be dropped to the vertical position to enable the screw coupling to be placed over the buckeye draw hook. The vertical position with the buffers extended was also necessary when the carriage was used at either end of a train or when stabled. The buckeye was secured in its horizontal or upright position for automatic coupling to another buckeye-fitted carriage by a support pin which the shunter slid into position. The support pin had a hinged tail piece at its end which shunters were required to make certain was in the down position to ensure the pin would not slide out as a result of oscillation when the train was moving. If the pin slid out the coupling would drop to the vertical position and the train become divided.

For many years it was always assumed that when such a division occurred it was due to the shunter not ensuring the tail piece was fully in the down position and he was dealt with under the disciplinary procedures until one day in the 1970s when a support pin was found to be partially out on a royal train at Ely.

Royal trains were a regular occurrence on the Kings Lynn to Liverpool Street line for royal visits to and from Sandringham, and each train was meticulously examined by both operating staff and carriage and wagon engineers to ensure it was fully in order. These examinations were carried out not only by the local staff but also checked by senior representatives from regional headquarters. It was therefore inconceivable that this particular buckeye pin had not had its tail piece properly placed in the down position at the start of the royal journey and therefore it must now be assumed these pins could work out with oscillation even with the tail piece down. An immediate modification was made to all buckeye support pins by fitting them with two hinged tail pieces of different lengths and weights to ensure they could not swing with oscillation into the horizontal position at the same time and thus allow the pin to start working its way out.

Another embarrassing incident occurred at Ely some years later and involved the serving of the Queen's breakfast. As explained in an early piece, the vestibule doors at the end of each carriage are fitted with external locks known as French pins or tower bolts. These can only be unlocked from outside and it is the shunter's duty to undo these locks immediately before coupling two carriages together, otherwise the doors cannot be opened from inside the vehicle

It was regular practice for members of the royal family to travel in royal or specially prepared carriages attached to normal service trains. On this occasion when the royal portion of the train had been attached to the service train at Kings Lynn the external vestibule door locks had not been undone. The result was that the chief steward could not get through the train to the royal carriage to serve the Queen's breakfast and he had to resort to carrying it down the platform when the train stopped at Ely.

Needless to say the press made much of this story, which rather proved George Goodings, the well-respected divisional manager at Norwich, to have been right with his advice to give newshounds a wide berth so as not to have to explain when things went wrong.

Let's Have a Party

Geoff Body was closely involved with railway party and excursion business at one time or another. With a contribution from his son Ian, he records a few memories of this varied activity.

Throughout most of their history railways have been keen to attract revenue from people who do not need to use their trains but might be encouraged to do so by the provision of special facilities and attractive fares. They spread their net wide and sought to stimulate travel by every conceivable type of special-interest group and to a great host and variety of special locations and events. Many of the latter, like the combined rail and steamers trips, were devised in the offices of the passenger section of the various district and divisional managers' offices or suggested by the canvassers who urged businesses and groups to trust their special occasion outing to the railway.

The inflated demand for passenger coaches at peak times meant that there was a great deal of capacity to be filled on other days. The keenness to attract more business may have led one young man responsible for party business to be

more trusting of his colleagues than was prudent. Ned, as we shall call him, and his deputy took turns to accompany any important Sunday excursion trains. These two were on the best of terms, did their jobs well but sometimes leavened the burden of making complicated arrangements by indulging in a little humour.

Unsuspecting, Ned was delighted with a letter purporting to be from a large naturist association and expressing interest in taking a trainload of delegates to an important conference in the Midlands. The date requested was one when Ned himself would be accompanying the train and with timings, the

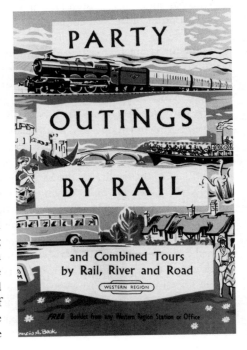

PARTY OUTINGS BY RAIL

and Combined Tours
by Rail, River and Road

WESTERN REGION

FREE Booklet from any Western Region Station or Office

availability of stock, crews and paths provisionally established he saw no reason not to make a positive reply to the enquiry. All then went forward smoothly until the colleagues behind the practical joke sent another letter, on the same convincing but entirely spurious headed notepaper, asking if there would be any objection to the intending passengers travelling without clothes while on the train. Since it was a private event and no one else would be affected. Ned eventually agreed.

Any misgivings Ned might have had then lay dormant until the arrival of yet another letter. This suggested that, as a gesture of respect for the organisers and the nature of the event, the accompanying railwayman might also remove his clothes for the journey. It was felt, said the writer, that this course would prevent any embarrassment he might feel at being the odd man out! Ned's consternation was so painful to watch that his colleagues could no longer keep straight faces and duly confessed to their deception, but it was a long time before they let their boss forget that he had been completely taken in by this imaginative prank.

All this happened in BR's West of England Division but in no way distracted from the passenger section's dedication to its business results. In 1968, for example, 1,136 parties were carried earning £55,898 but a year later the numbers had risen further to 1,412 parties producing £69,221 in revenue. The full train load business increased too, partly due to a contract with travel agents Renwicks Travel Ltd who hired twenty-seven trains which they would fill with passengers from South Devon to special events in London.

A focal point of the West of England Division was Bristol Temple Meads station.

Beside the rising approach road to this modern station the original GWR terminus still stands, but at the period under notice the old roadside offices were used only for the storage of old files of papers, thousands and thousands of them. Most of this long-forgotten correspondence concerned claims matters but I unearthed one batch of old handbills which proved to relate to excursions which had operated many years ago.

The practice then was for each station to send a copy of the relevant advertising handbill to the GWR district superintendent with a summary of the response to the facility on the back. One such example, from Castle Cary, recorded that an excursion to Weymouth was completely full when it arrived there and the waiting passengers had to be accommodated by fetching a parcels van from the yard and putting the seats from the station platform inside. The final comment 'Some passengers reported an eventful journey' seemed a massive understatement about what must have occurred as the train snaked down through the curves from Evershot summit!

The Division also had its own programme of 'Mystery Trains'. People seemed to like the surprise of not knowing where they were going and the regular summer Mystery Trains had a large and faithful following. Among them was a lovely couple who decided to celebrate their ruby wedding on one of these trains and were quite overwhelmed when we presented them with a special commemorative cake on the journey to Newquay and the local television people appeared to record the occasion. Another popular train outing was the sequence of 'Monkey Specials' that brought passengers from South Wales to Clifton Down station and the delights of nearby Bristol Zoo.

All over the country securing optional business kept the staff of the passenger business on their toes. Rail and steamer trips were especially popular, whether it be from Glasgow down the Clyde or by rail to Totnes, on to Dartmouth by paddle steamer and then back home from Kingswear station. Another popular Devon circular tour facility was the 1s 6d excursion from Exeter to Starcross, by steam launch from there to Exmouth and back by train to the starting point. From 1 June each summer there was also a circular tour of 'Romantic Dartmoor' from Paignton or Torquay, costing 5s 6d and described thus:

> Proceeding via Bickington and Ramshorn Down to Haytor Rocks, where there will be a wait of 2.5 hours for Lunch, and to allow passengers to view the Rocks and other places of interest. The car proceeds at 2.00p.m by White Gate, Jay's Grave, Heatree and Manaton to BECKY FALLS where a wait of half-an-hour will be allowed, returning thence at 3.30p.m. via Trendlebeer Down and Bovey Tracey.

Many a WI group enjoyed a rail journey to Reading, lunch in the Co-op restaurant and then tea on the Thames on board one of Salter's period steamers. Agricultural shows, London events, the Blackpool Illuminations, firms' outings and music festivals all brought extra passengers to the railway, demanding the careful planning of trains and crews, finding train paths, laying on refreshments and careful cooperation with the destination event people and any other parties involved in ensuring the passengers had a really enjoyable day out.

Of course, not everything always ran according to plan. A small staff group to which I belonged organised a small party for an outing by ordinary train from Liverpool Street to Yarmouth South Town from which point we then continued over the old Norfolk & Suffolk Joint Committee route to Lowestoft, a journey remarkable for the swing bridge crossing of Breydon Water. After a stop at Lowestoft to wander round the fish market we returned in the portion of a train which would be joined at Beccles with a second portion which had originated at Yarmouth.

It had been an interesting but tiring day and the decision to get several beers from the buffet car before the Yarmouth lot swamped it seemed a wise one. The various bottles and glasses were all on the table when the two train portions were united, rather more forcibly than they should have been. The entire liquid supply was tipped into my lap creating a level of wet discomfort that proved to be the least of my problems. If I stirred from my seat every passenger's nose twitched and every eye examined me furtively. Time did little to ease my embarrassment and crossing Liverpool Street to my Enfield train in that peculiar stiff-limbed walk affected by people with damp trousers made the day even more memorable by the sheer volume of interest it appeared to attract. Or perhaps I was just too self-conscious.

A more auspicious occasion occurred a few years later, in 1961. At that time the Caledonian Steam Packet Company was in the habit of inviting railway staff concerned with promoting party business to spend three days as their guests to see what their steamers and the resorts west of Glasgow had to offer. It was a sound idea and no doubt helped to stimulate more group business for both the railway and the steamer company.

The tour took place in September and was extremely comprehensive, embracing such places as Balloch, Loch Lomond, Ardlui, Rothesay, the Kyles of Bute, Dunoon, Arran, Cumbrae and Ardrossan. The travel logistics were impeccable but there was no overall plan for hospitality and each place, hotel, provost and tourist agency visited was left to make their own arrangements. No one stinted, so that breakfast at the main hotel was followed by another on the steamer, morning coffee, drinks and lunch on board before alighting at, say, Brodick, yet another lunch after the bus tour round the island and then tea on the returning steamer. Each hotel visited wanted to ply us with its best whisky and the same happened after the evening meal and throughout the 'typical Scottish entertainment' provided into the late hours.

The places we visited were beautiful, the people charming and their hospitality warm and generous. All who went could vouch for the benefits of party travel to this area of Scotland but few would have had the stamina to continue the jaunt beyond the three days allocated.

The Day War Broke Out

Bill Parker reflects on a very enjoyable special event that would probably have health and safety restrictions today.

After a somewhat chequered history, the diversionary line from Hertford North to Langley Junction stumbled back into full use by stopping passenger trains with the station at Watton-at-Stone being formally reopened by Sir Peter Parker. Sir Nigel Gresley's home had been here and at one period had been used by the LNER as a training school. Now, with significant funding from county, district and parish councils, the station was back in business.

Enjoying their day out, local school children wait for their train journey part in the opening of Watton-at-Stone station in Hertfordshire.

The station had been closed at the outbreak of the Second World War and the reopening ceremony began, appropriately, with a dialect version of comedian Rob Wilton's '*The day war broke out…*'. Children from local schools lined the Up platform and provided music for the occasion. They then had a ride to Hertford North station and back on the Class 313 unit that 'broke the tape' to signify the station open. Quite a lot of adults joined the trip and the media was well represented, all creating good public relations and introducing youngsters to train travel.

In retrospect, with so many children present and no barriers along the edge of the platform or other special security measures, Bill has great doubts about whether such an event would be possible today.

Britannias Versus V2s

Whilst understanding the practical merits of the various classes of locomotive, most railwaymen cherished a special affection for one particular design. David Ward remembers some opinions.

Staff morale in East Anglia was greatly lifted when the new BR Standard Class 4-6-2 Britannia locomotives replaced the various ageing 4-6-0s on the Norwich main line. With some lively performances the speed and reliability of services improved greatly and the reaction of passengers was very positive. And as that doyen of railway operators Gerry Fiennes put it, referring to the dividends in terms of productive use of rolling stock and train crews, 'The faster you go, the cheaper you go.'

There was, however, a price to be paid. Norwich shedmaster Bill Harvey had to manage the increased maintenance costs resulting from eight years of intensive running and problems like frame fractures and bulges in the copper firebox. He observed, 'Like racehorses, it is the pace that kills.'

In the early Britannia years John Bramwell was chief mechanical foreman at Norwich shed. Later on, when the 1936 pioneer V2 2-6-2 *Green Arrow* was being restored there, he was asked whether he would have preferred a fleet of V2s or a similar number of Britannias in his care. Pithily he commented, 'V2s would have run the trains just as well and been half the trouble.'

Kings Cross top link driver Bill Hoole judged the Britannia a good locomotive but believed that they could not have stood up to the punishment that V2s took during the war.

Collapse of the Ness Bridge

John Ellis describes the dramatic events in February 1989 when the flood waters of the River Ness washed away the Inverness rail bridge used by the vital train service to Kyle of Lochalsh and the far northern parts of the Highland Region.

I was general manager of Scotrail Region from September 1987 until January 1990. On 6 February 1989, I travelled to Inverness for a meeting with Highland Regional Council the following day. There had been a huge amount of rain in the North East and I was told that the River Ness was in full spate. In the evening I went down to the river, and it was lapping the embankments and running at a fearsome rate. The Ness has the steepest fall of any river in the country, and it was certainly evident.

The following morning I was having breakfast in the hotel (porridge and kippers of course!) when an ashen-faced Ronnie Munro, the Inverness station manager, came in to tell us that the rail bridge had been washed away. When I went down to look, the rails were suspended above the raging river, with no sign of the bridge spans.

There was obviously great concern locally that the bridge would not be replaced. I had a hectic morning of telephone calls with Board HQ and

The railway bridge route across the River Ness with piers and track devastated by its flood waters. (G. Smith/Jim Summers Collection)

many others, and was able to get a verbal agreement that the bridge would be replaced. I therefore arranged a press conference that afternoon to make this announcement. This was to ensure that there were no second thoughts at Board HQ, in the Other Provincial Services business sector, or in the Department of Transport!

Then followed all of the decisions, debates and arguments about what we should do about train services to the Far North and Kyle of Lochalsh; what the design of the new bridge should be; and how to deal with a claim for damages from the Harbour Board due to the debris from the bridge blocking the harbour!

It was agreed to operate a rail shuttle service over the two isolated routes, with a bus connection from Inverness, planning for a long blockage which would include a considerable summer timetable change. It also required, *inter alia*, an extensive exchange of rolling stock by road haulage between the areas, and creation of a temporary maintenance depot at Muir of Ord. The following piece by Jim Summers explains most comprehensively the planning considerations and their implementation, which produced very successful results.

It was eventually agreed to rebuild the Ness Bridge on a like-for-like basis, rather than a modern (and quicker) steel structure. At last the work was completed and rail services were restored in 2000.

An Independent Railway

Based on a paper he read to the Annual Summer Convention of the Permanent Way Institution in Edinburgh in 1990, sometime BR Scotland Regional Operations Manager Jim Summers elaborates on the Ness Bridge situation.

Locomotives travelling along our motorways on the backs of lorries are a common sight nowadays, but it was not always thus. The art was perfected in the far north of Scotland during a remarkable period when the national network was cut off from the old Highland Railway lines north and west of Inverness. For the railway folk involved, there was certainly never a dull moment after they found they were required to run a mini-network all on its own. It all came about when a passer-by reported on the morning of Tuesday 7 February 1989 that the viaduct carrying the railway north of Inverness appeared no longer to be functional. The precise entries in the control office log began as follows:

08.28 – Fire Service HQ Inverness reports advice from a member of the public that the rail bridge across the river at Shore Street has collapsed into the river, and a car is en-route to investigate.

08.30 – RETB confirms line blocked to traffic.

08.33 – Civil Police confirm that the central span of the Ness Bridge has collapsed.

By 08.40 the log was recording the alterations fixed for the trains already on the move. The Control action had been swift and decisive. Dingwall had been agreed as the most convenient point to turn services. The morning Up trains from Wick/Thurso and Kyle of Lochalsh were not far away at the time of the disaster, but buses had been arranged from Dingwall and the passengers actually arrived in Inverness on time.

The collapse of the bridge was a progressive affair, and a subsequent string of doleful messages reported the collapse of further arches. It was an awesome situation to face – a mini-system, known for its remoteness and lack of profitability, was now cut off from the umbilical cord of the national network. But this story tells how professional ingenuity and optimism won through, and how all departments played their part.

The control office in Glasgow had produced an initial 'first aid' response, and the Area folk were coping very well. However, the social/political implications of the event were obviously going to be far-reaching. Yet within the overall misfortune of the collapse, a number of elements of good fortune could be discerned. One such element was the arrival in Inverness of the ScotRail general manager to find he had a crisis on his hands, and the media were not going to forego this golden opportunity to establish just what the long-term implications were. He took the pressure off the front-line managers.

Another piece of good fortune was the hour of the collapse, since it occurred when the maximum amount of rolling stock was on the north side of the break. The morning Down trains had crossed the viaduct, but the Up trains had not yet crossed it into Inverness. This gave six locomotives and sixteen coaches marooned on the north side – enough to sustain the timetabled passenger service. Crews, cleaning, fuelling, maintenance were needed as well, and all were normally centred in Inverness. Train crew rosters were accordingly reconstructed to incorporate not only a road trip from and to their depot, but also the preparation and disposal of locomotives at, initially, Dingwall, but subsequently Muir of Ord. Cleaning staff and maintenance staff likewise were re-arranged to carry out their work, day and night, on the north side. Messrooms and facilities had to be established. Fuelling was arranged by road.

Back in Glasgow that morning, engineers, operators and business managers were meeting to discuss how to sustain the services until the bridge was rebuilt. Even that was not a foregone conclusion; loss-making rural lines do not easily attract substantial investment when resources are scarce. It was clear that the interim arrangements were going to have to last for a very long time. Thus the first stage, a fairly ruthless response to the crisis, had to be refined. This meant decisions on how we were going to house the staff and the maintenance of the marooned rolling stock. The fitters had been performing wonders in appalling weather conditions, lying under locomotives and carriages out in the open with snow falling.

For the rolling stock maintenance in the longer term, the use of the effectively closed Muir of Ord station was an early choice. Prospecting revealed the possibility of transferring the former construction depot building used for the Ayrshire electrification from Barassie. Requirements for a pit, concrete area and so on were early established, and the investment case proceeded apace. Obviously a high degree of self-sufficiency was implicit and, in the event, accident repairs and bogie changes were routinely carried out. This self-sufficiency had also to include the civil engineer, who would need ballast trains and other facilities in the separated network.

Some traffic consequences were less immediately obvious: the blocking of the harbour by the fallen masonry turned out to mean the railway had prevented the supply of oil to the distribution depot at Inverness by coastwise shipping. An alternative rail service from Grangemouth was substituted.

The train services had been concentrated on Dingwall, because it was the junction for the Kyle and Wick/Thurso lines, and also had easy road access from Inverness. The A9 road and the Kessock bridge, opened only a few years before, proved to be a key factor, and another piece of good fortune. Normally when buses have to be substituted for trains on part of a route, an extension of journey time is implicit. Clearly this can destroy connections at junctions, and Inverness is a focal point for the trunk connections to/from the south. Compared with that new road however, the railway between Inverness and Dingwall is circuitous, so that the substitute buses could match the rail times, even allowing for the additional transfer times. A van was provided for passengers' luggage, and parcels traffic, very important in that part of the world. The journey times proved unsuitable in the high season for including a detour to call at the intermediate station of Muir of Ord, and so a separate vehicle was organised.

The arrangements at Dingwall were not ideal for passengers, since the economical track work arrangements under RETB involved sprung points and loop facilities designed to permit trains to cross one another. To facilitate the interchange for passengers between road and rail, and avoid use of the footbridge, the points were altered to lie in such a manner that Up and Down trains could be handled at the main platform. Changes in trackwork were also made at Muir of Ord, which involved delicate negotiations with tenants in the former goods yard.

The high season always brings a significant increase in rail traffic to the Highlands, around eight-fold compared with winter. Not only were additional coaches required, but a programme of high-quality land cruise trains emanated each year from major traffic centres in England and had to be taken into account. Indeed fifty-four trains had operated over the season in 1988. This all had to figure in the consolidation of the emergency arrangements for the longer term and the planning for the future. And was there to be a future at all?

This is not the place to describe the decision-making which led to the resolve to rebuild the bridge. Suffice to say that the general manager was able to announce in Inverness at around lunch-time on that first day that it would indeed be rebuilt. This was a public relations achievement of deep importance to the community and staff alike, and says much for the speed of decision-making possible in the nationalised railway.

Meanwhile the little group in the regional operations manager's room was facing an extra factor in the forthcoming summer. The summer timetable, due to commence in May, featured the cut-over to diesel multiple units. It can be rightly inferred that the existing loco-hauled rolling stock was therefore not in the best of condition. Nor was it capable of operating the accelerated and improved timetable envisaged under the Super Sprinter operation. Such a commitment of brand new resources to these lines, along with the recent investment in the modern RETB signalling, had been a most meaningful demonstration to the community of ScotRail's commitment to them.

The little group resolved, without argument, that the new Super Sprinter service would have to be introduced somehow. It was aware of the essential requirement south of the border for the locomotives due to be released by Sprinters; and there were other cascading effects crucial to the national business strategy. By willing the end, though, the little group had to will the means of getting the rolling stock over the Firth, in both directions.

That was the strategy, but meantime other tactical matters needed to be addressed, such as improving the finer points of the bus operation, and the eleventh-hour alteration of the public rail timetables to reflect the bus connections. A really serious concern though was how to ensure that everyone knew that ScotRail was still in business north of Inverness. The leisure market is very fickle, and much business could be lost by any misunderstanding, so it was depressing to find that, even in Scotland, members of the public thought that Inverness had been cut off from the South and that, in effect, rail services had totally ceased. Heavy publicity, coinciding with the movement of the new Sprinter vehicles to the separated railway, helped to remind our colleagues further away, and the public generally, that we were still very much in business

The traction & rolling stock engineer was active and ingenious in finding means of transferring stock across the Firth, and was sustained by the enthusiasm of the British Railways Board, and even the chairman himself, from the very first day of the decision. It is literally true that some investigation was made of airlifting vehicles, but in the event, road haulage was chosen with a loading point at Inverness yard and unloading at Invergordon. The movement was two-way, since the old stock, including certain freight vehicles, had to be moved out and new Super Sprinters taken across. Snowploughs also made the trip.

Additionally, an exchange of coaching stock was necessary, since it had been resolved by InterCity Charters that the high-quality land cruise train facility should continue to be offered. This significant act of confidence involved the transfer of refurbished MK1 vehicles, equipped to a high standard of luxury. In the event twenty-six special trains were run. The popular observation car was also to be operated for locally based tourists, and so this converted dmu power car also had to be transferred along with the 'Heritage Train', which was the loco-hauled summer extra train aimed at the tourist market and painted in a special livery during the winter. It can be justly inferred from all this that the Scottish system of area management had been working well at Inverness in its intended role as a mini-business, with delegated commercial and operating authority.

The road movements were carefully arranged in association with the police to avoid times of heavy road use, but it was ironical that the initial movement, eagerly awaited by the media, was delayed by the failure of a road vehicle on its journey north. One journey was also nullified by shoppers' cars blocking access. The first series of movements set up the summer service with the new Sprinters and the summer tourist trains. A second set of transfers took place for the winter service, and locomotive exchanges were getting rolling stock over the Firth in both directions.

The schedule of movements involved was as follows:
April 1989 (a) Northbound 6 x Class 156 Super Sprinters, 7 x InterCity charter coaches, 8 x Provincial 'Heritage' coaches. (b) Southbound 10 x BP tanks, 3 x Polybulks, 2 x Class 37 locomotives.
October 1989 (a) Northbound 2 x snowploughs, 3 x Class 37 locomotives, 1 x Provincial coach. (b) Southbound 4 x Class 37 locomotives, 7 x InterCity charter coaches, 10 x Provincial coaches.

It is good to have the opportunity of this book to record for posterity the outstanding efforts of the fitters, carriage cleaners, station staff, civil engineers, traincrews and the many others who enabled the independent 'Network North' to operate smoothly and effectively from the first day. Incidentally, the gales of the following week caused far more havoc in operating terms and required greater attention to overcome. The viaduct collapse was spectacular for the media, but to the operators was no more than a line blockage, to be worked around while the engineers put things right.

Happily, passenger loading figures were sustained during the year of separation, and the lines operated with some of the finest timekeeping figures in the whole of ScotRail. And the even happier ending was that the new viaduct opened successfully and was built to take locomotives, despite siren voices suggesting that all that would ever be needed in the far North would be lightweight diesel multiple units.

Flying the Flag

Mike Lamport realised quite early on that he wanted a career in railway public relations. By persistence he achieved it and, from his many appointments, reaped a rich harvest of experiences of which these are just a few examples.

A Brush with Crime
One morning in 1970 when I worked in the British Rail Travel Centre in London's Regent Street I had just filled the racks of pocket timetables that lined the wall opposite the Thomas Cook Bureau de Change when I noticed

BR chairman Peter Parker being interviewed by a BBC *Look North* reporter at the opening of the new HST depot at Heaton, Newcastle-upon-Tyne, on 7 November 1977, with the inimitable 'Informed Source' Roger Ford looking on.

The author's final encounter with the much admired and respected leader came in 1983 as, for the last time as chairman, he headed back to London on the Yorkshire Pullman. Mike comments, 'I had a few moments with him to introduce myself and thank him for all he had done for the industry and for me, a PR man. His typically warm and personal response was, "Ah, so that's who you are. I have often seen you in the background and now I know why you were there!"' (Mike Lamport)

that two men were loitering about the racks and patently pretending to look for a pocket table. As I was pointing this out to a colleague one of the men suddenly produced a baseball bat and proceeded to club the bureau manager over the back of the head, forcing him to drop the cash box which had been kept overnight in the main office safe.

After the men had fled, falling over themselves in the street as they grappled with the weighty box, I ran over to the poor man as he lay on the floor and stupidly asked 'Are you alright?' Silly thing to say and his reply was not really repeatable but fortunately he was not injured, only shocked like the rest of us who had witnessed the attack.

The rest of the day was spent both in Savile Row police station and later in the Criminal Record Bureau at New Scotland Yard where we were encouraged to leaf through volumes of photos of known villains.

I gather that the men were eventually apprehended for another crime and confessed to this one, so at least I was spared another day in court. I had already been through that ordeal after I apprehended a sneak thief who, a few months earlier, had calmly walked in through the staff entrance and happily helped himself to the contents of the jackets that we had discarded in favour of our rather cheap and nasty grey linen-like uniform blazers. My evidence, given in the witnessbox at Bow Street Magistrates Court, saw the thief duly punished, but I had no wish ever again to be cross-examined by a defence counsel!

Dressing the Part

One day, just after I had started working in the LMR headquarters press office, Eric White the assistant public relations officer called me into his inner sanctum. There he asked if I thought I was up to 'managing' a photo-shoot which he had arranged to capture a series of pictures to accompany a press release reminding all that this year saw the centenary of the Lake Windermere steamers. I replied in the affirmative, while inside wondering quite what I had let myself in for, and went home to tell my parents that I was going to be away for a night next week in the company of a photographer and a couple of photographic female models! So this is what public relations is all about I thought!

The day came and the four for us duly set off from Euston on a rather grey late spring day and, whilst I was naturally excited to be in such glamorous company, Eric's instruction that I should contact the hotel manager on my arrival to collect the top hat and frock coat that he wanted me to wear in the photo-shoot was causing me some concern. He had decided that I should quickly learn that the job was not always about watching over things; sometimes you could be called upon to participate!

Late that afternoon we arrived at the Newby Bridge Hotel near Bowness where the manager, who turned out to be a part-time magician, handed me his frock coat, top hat, waistcoat and trousers and wished me well with the next day's shoot. Fortunately he and I were both slim and 6ft, but however I dressed I still looked like a 'Seventies' man with my overlong hair and slightly drooping moustache.

Morning came and we were given the good ship *Tern* to act as our prop, moored against the pier at Lakeside. When the two ladies emerged in all their Victorian finery they added much-needed colour to the still grey day, although I was feeling less than comfortable in my borrowed outfit.

Nonetheless the railway photographer 'John' was a master of his art and he soon set about getting the poses right against the backgrounds that Eric had indicated he wanted recorded. All went well until John needed to get a wider angle shot of the two ladies, so he and I stood together as he leant out over the rail of the vessel to frame the shot. It was then he somehow lost his grip on the camera and to our joint horror he and I watched as the £600 Hasselblad slipped from his grasp and, in what felt like slow motion, fell into the deep! Although the camera and the most recent shots were lost, John quickly produced another camera and, seemingly unfazed by the loss of the treasured tool of his trade, finished the assignment in time for us to change and board the train back to London along with our haul of pictures.

A Royal Request

One of the more unusual of the many requests made to public relations offices that I have worked in came in the form of a phone call from the *Birmingham Evening Mail* in 1973. They wanted their readers to be able to see full-colour pictures of the morning wedding of HRH Princess Anne and Captain Mark Phillips at Westminster Abbey in that evening's edition, and asked if it would be possible to find some space on one of our Birmingham-bound trains where a photographic darkroom could be set up? Keen to help as ever, we eventually settled on their exclusive use of the leading BG of a train which duly departed with an eager darkroom crew setting to work almost immediately on the arrival of the breathless photographers. Thanks to our joint efforts the good people of the West Midlands were that evening treated to high-quality full-colour pictures of the Royal Wedding.

Off the Menu

Even being an 'on call' press officer brought its lighter moments, including the time when I got a message from our divisional control office in Preston tipping me off that I might get a call from the press about the sorry tale of the missing main course on that day's Midday Scot! My informant reported that, following an altercation at the buffet bar, a rather inebriated passenger who had been refused another drink got his own back by barging into the adjacent kitchen where he snatched the ready-to-carve chicken from the chef and promptly threw it out of the window onto the Cumbrian Fells!

High Speed Hiccups

Despite their obvious success, the introduction of InterCity 125s on the Eastern Region was not without its teething problems, and we had to work hard to counter tales of toilets that 'blew back' on their hapless users and the outer glazing of carriage windows that were sucked out as trains passed each other at full speed. Neither of these phenomena had been experienced by our Western Region counterparts as the wider distance between tracks afforded by the reduction of the original broad gauge had avoided the potential for the air pressure 'bombs' that were created on the fastest stretches of the East Coast Main Line.

Rural Ways

On one occasion I agreed to a request from a feature writer on the *Northern Echo* newspaper to ride in the brake van of the then freight-only Wensleydale branch from Northallerton to Redmire, but only on the strict understanding

SIGNAL BOX COMING UP, SIR!

that he would not report <u>all</u> that he saw! When, after reading the newspaper article, the chief freight manager queried why he was paying signalmen to mend cycles and repair watches, a glance at the receipts for the line quickly silenced him. What he didn't know, and the journalist could not report, was that the freight train oft times provided an unofficial market-day passenger service for the wives of railway staff at crossing keepers' cottages along the way, and was also the scene of regular rabbit shoots!

Thought Provoking

David Crathorn recounts a dramatic moment in the workaday life of Orpington signal box.

In 1947, or thereabouts, a schoolboy who was very interested in railways and particularly in the electric traction of trains and railway signalling lived not far from Orpington signal box. Whenever he could he would go to the box and if he was invited in he would spend hours there. Generally he just stood observing the working, but some of the signalmen would ask him to move a lever if they were engaged at the other end of the box.

One very foggy evening the young man was standing at the London end of Orpington signal box, having been there for several hours. The signalman signalled a terminating train from London into the Down Bay platform. The train duly arrived and came to a stand, clear of the Down Main Line.

For no reason, without a word from the signalman, the lad moved the point lever leading to the bay back in the frame.

Before anything could be done, out of the fog from Petts Wood burst a double-headed boat train at speed and ran safely over the unlocked facing connection, having passed all signals at danger at Petts Wood.

The lad went on to be a highly respected railway signal engineer. He never forgot the Orpington incident.

The interior of a traditional signal box, in this case Dr Days Bridge Junction at Bristol.

Glossary

ASLEF	Associated Society of Locomotive Engineers & Firemen
ASM	Assistant Station Master
AYM	Assistant Yard Master
BRB	British Railways Board
BRS	British Road Services
BT	British Transport
C&W	Carriage & Wagon
dmu	Diesel Multiple Unit
emu	Electric Multiple Unit
ER	Eastern Region (of British Rail)
GLC	Greater London Council
GN&GE	Great Northern & Great Eastern
GPO	General Post Office
GWR	Great Western Railway
HST	High Speed Train
LDDC	London Docklands Development Corporation
LMR	London Midland Region (of British Rail)
LMS	London, Midland & Scottish Railway
LNER	London & North Eastern Railway
LNWR	London & North Western Railway
M&GN	Midland & Great Northern
Met	Metropolitan (Police)
NBR	North British Railway
NER	North Eastern Railway
REME	Royal Mechanical & Electrical Engineers
RETB	Radio Electronic Token Block
TA	Traffic Apprentice
TUCC	Transport Users Consultative Committee

Railway Rolling Stock:

In normal daily operation different types of coaches, vans and wagons were referred to by abbreviated terms used to classify and describe them. These abbreviations were generally related to the function of the vehicle concerned; for example, a CCT was a covered carriage truck, and a GUV was a general utility van for parcels etc by passenger train. Carriage 'codes' used two-letter combinations which gave an indication of the purpose served e.g. an S indicated second class, K served for a dual-class carriage, B indicated a brake compartment and so on. Special-purpose freight wagons included the 'Platefit', a vacuum brake-fitted flat wagon for carrying steel plate etc; 'Bobol,' a bogie wagon with bolsters for carrying long steelwork; and Lowmac, a wagon with a low centre section to facilitate the carriage of machinery. An ISO container was one built to international standards, BD containers used to be the normal unit where road to rail transfers were involved, and Presflos were high-capacity wagons introduced for the carriage of cement in bulk.